Storytelling with Children

Published by Hawthorn Press, Hawthorn House, 1 Lansdown Lane, Stroud, Gloucestershire, GL5 1BJ, UK
Tel: (01453) 757040 Fax: (01453) 751138
www.hawthornpress.com

Permission granted to quote from:
Louise MacNeice Collected Poems, Faber and Faber
Illustrations by Marije Rowling
Cover illustration by Siân Bailey
Cover Design by Jennie Hoare, River Design, Bradford on Avon, Wiltshire.
Typesetting by Hawthorn Press, Stroud, Gloucestershire.
Printed in the UK by The Cromwell Press, Trowbridge, Wiltshire.

Reprinted by The Cromwell Press, 2001

British Library Cataloguing in Publication Data applied for

ISBN 1 903458 08 0

Storytelling with Children.

Nancy Mellon

Foreword by Thomas Moore

Hawthorn Press

*This book is lovingly dedicated to Hugh
(Brother Blue) and Ruth Hill,
close friends of the Eternal Storyteller,
and to aspiring storytellers everywhere.*

Contents

Foreword

by Thomas Moore

Five years ago I began telling stories to my two children in the half-hour before they went to sleep. I didn't do this on principle or theory. It just happened. Many of the stories have become quite long with episodes complete in themselves told over months and even years. They often begin with a formula and contain common structural elements. The same characters appear, and new faces show themselves. For example, the series about King Francis and Queen Maeve frequently begins with King Francis waking early in the morning and going to the balcony just off his bedroom to look over his kingdom. Everything is usually still and beautiful except one little anomaly that usually appears faintly on the horizon.

Every night I ask my children which story they'd like to hear. They say 'King Francis' or 'Ananda Coomeraswamy' or 'Blue Foot.' Sometimes they tell me what they want to have in the story, but I usually tell them that I can't force the characters or the story to do what I want. I listen to the story being offered to us as much as they do.

I've learned a great deal over the years from this storytelling. I've discovered the beauty of repetition and formula, the power of a character to become a person in our field of relationships, and the arc a good story covers whether it is long or short. First I almost always take a moment of silence to let the evening's story be born and show itself in the sketchiest form. I've learned to trust that a story will take form and complete itself if I'm open to inspiration. The few friends who know about this storytelling tell me how good it is for the children, but I do not think of it in those terms. It's pure pleasure, and it's something the children and I have discovered that we can do with each other. Many an evening I'm grateful that even when the story doesn't pass muster in my judgment, they are happy and appreciative. When a story is done, I hear them stir from their deep attention and shift into a different world to prepare for sleep. The sounds of that moment are the sweetest music in my life. Very rarely do the children fall asleep while the story is being told, although when they do I am happy for that.

I know firsthand how precious and pleasurable family storytelling can be. I want to underscore the point that this tradition in our family simply sprang into being. I didn't initiate it out of any philosophy of education or upbringing. I do happen to have many ideas and theories about stories, but somehow they have been involved only unconsciously.

And so I'm delighted with this new book by Nancy Mellon on storytelling for parents. She, too, has many ideas but she presents them without any annoying theory. She can appreciate many variations in the practice and the mode of stores told. She helps articulate what is possible by letting us know what in fact is done in families. At the same time she helps us see how family stories can have classic themes and forms. She understands the importance of voice and articulation, but she doesn't offer rules.

I think her book will give parents guidance and courage to trust their imaginations and to explore certain simple structural motifs common to great stories and the simple ones that arrive on a parent's lips on an ordinary evening. The last thing we parents need is a rule book for storytelling. What we can use is some gentle encouragement to adopt the persona of storyteller. I appreciate Nancy Mellon's way of giving us good ideas without making us feel that we are now bound to certain expectations of what is right and proper. Once the pleasure and personal inventiveness leave the process, we've lost the heart and soul of this kind of storytelling.

The parent who is a storyteller enters a tradition that looks simple but is actually complex and serious. Family storytelling is more than kid's stuff. Its pleasures are fully adult for the storyteller. All of this Nancy Mellon describes with a good storyteller's sensitivity. She also mentions the obstacles that parents run into as they try to tell stories. Sometimes, I admit, I'm afraid that my stories won't seem good enough, but that's the writer and academic in me raising voices of unnecessary caution.

At the deepest level of experience, our lives are made up of story fragments and images in search of a coherent narrative. We find meaning in those stories. The deeper we go into them, the deeper the place from which we live. It follows, I would say, that storytelling is the primary task of the parent. Making stories honest, attractive and appropriate for children is an inviting task. Reading stories has its extraordinary pleasures and value, but 'making up' stories – letting them come to you – is the best kind of storytelling I know.

When I do step back and think about my practice of family storytelling, one hope I have for my children is that they are discovering how to be in this life with imagination. The kingdom of King Francis and Queen Maeve and the curiosity shop of Ananda Coomeraswamy are real. They're imaginary, but to me the imaginary is in many ways more vital than so-called 'reality' – life deprived of imagination. Let Nancy Mellon teach you to be a storyteller and a discoverer, for you and your children, of worlds that truly make a difference.

Introduction

It is a blessing to have a wise and dedicated storyteller in the family, and it is never too early or too late to become one.

For countless generations storytelling has provided vision and consolation, inspiration and instruction; yet our present times demand new approaches and dedication to this ancient art. This book can help you discover why and how to become a family storyteller, and to transform any reluctance you have, so that storytelling may thrive in your life with your children.

Although children often show us our shortcomings, as we devote ourselves to them they can inspire us to deeds we never thought possible. They learn from us to tap into the hidden riches of their memories and imaginations as we grow with them, in order to fulfill their needs.

Many parents and other adults are surprised at first that young children want them to make up stories out of themselves. Yet it does not take long to realize how meeting their need for stories creates a sense of warmth, family and community. This book has been written to stimulate your direct experience of the wise and benevolent creative forces which, however dormant they may be, live within every one of us. Computer stories, television, and even printed books are chilly substitutes for closeness with fully present adults who are spinning whole tales out of their own hearts and souls. Warmly creative adults inspire the same qualities in the children around them.

Amidst the ingenious cacophony of electronic inventions, the wise old art of storytelling is re-awakening with conscious intention. Many parents and grandparents feel a growing need to transform themselves into warm-hearted, fully present storytellers. As they tell their first stories to their children or grandchildren, or gather into story circles in villages, towns and cities to practice their favorite tales, they soon sense that everyone is a storyteller with an endless supply of personal and universal themes. Stories can draw from past, present and future cultures; through them we can discover ourselves in each other: the world-wide human family. As storytellers we can commune with our ancestors and rediscover our spiritual origins; we can tune to the wisdom of the natural world, and to the star-filled heavens. We can speak to the future through imagination—the language of evolution.

Parents and children both need to hear stories told aloud. One of my greatest joys over many years has been to develop the art of storytelling with families. Since I first discovered its creative power as a teacher of young children, I have met a great many people from diverse backgrounds and cultures who wanted to have more confidence in themselves as storytellers. In this book you will meet some of these adventuresome people, who began storytelling when their children were young or not yet born, with the puzzlement most of us experience when we begin unfamiliar activities. Yet lasting and abundant benefits have flowed back to them. I hope their creativity and courage will move you to become a more confident storyteller: for the children in your life, for your own sake, and for your larger community.

1 Weaving a Storyteller's Mantle

All things are connected ...
Chief Seattle, North American Indian

For love of stories, God made humanity.
Elie Wiesel

What is a Storyteller?

Babies, like storytellers, look into the world with wonder and surprise. They sense old and knowing ways of speech gathering about them. Between timelessness and time, they begin to draw words and images from a vast weave of sound and meaning. As children discover with delight this vibrant mantle of speech, memory and imagination that enfolds every human being, they insist we help draw it around them, sensing that only within it can they fully grow into their own humanity.

Becoming a storyteller in your family is an opportunity to develop a more conscious and sensitive relationship with the quality of your words and your tone of voice. With the same commitment you bring to providing wholesome meals, you can serve stories rich in words, images and spiritual content. As you let the genius and vitality of language flow through your voice, it will surely return to you through the children. Courageous beginners, they form their organs of speech through diligent practice, sometimes taking extraordinary risks to express themselves. Their spirit and desire to communicate can be your greatest inspiration: like a child, you can rediscover the wonderment of words.

Reading a book to a young child is a very different experience from telling a story. Parents often have their first liberation as storytellers from reading a satisfying story so often that it takes flight. Sensing a child's need to hear a story coming directly from them, it can be a great experience to break free of written words and speak a tale from memory.

Imagine a storyteller

There are many ways to become established in the oral tradition, whether or not there has been a storytelling tradition in your family. I often ask mothers and fathers to imagine a storyteller who will help them to communicate with their children. A frail young mother of four children pictured the storyteller as 'a stern American Indian, standing strong and upright. In her left hand she carries a beautifully carved staff that has been passed to her through generations. With a conch shell in her right hand she calls her people together when she has important stories to tell.' The mother recognized this storyteller to be a hidden part of herself that urgently wanted to help her speak with wisdom and authority to her children.

Another young mother discovered that she could invoke this wise old aspect of herself by beginning each of her stories with the same Slavic melody and the words:

Far away across the ocean, over the sunlit fields of golden hay, over villages with red-tiled roofs, far far beyond the mountains in the black forest, there lives an old woman. Her hair is pure white. There is a garland on her head. She sits in her old wooden chair and this is the story she tells...

This method has helped her on countless occasions. Of the old storyteller within, she says 'I trust her. She gives me strength when I am tired, or feeling impatient with the children. Always humming in her clearing, I picture her wrinkled face, her wisps of silvery hair, her old skirt. I see her seated, with grasses at her feet, surrounded by birds. It is as if the children and I journey to her in a swift balloon. By the time we arrive in her realm I feel more put together. We travel over fields of France, and over the tiled roofs of my Belgian ancestors, until we arrive in a clearing somewhere in eastern Europe. As I start to hum her melody, the children take a breath. It is as if all the generations of our family listen with us.'

A father of a three- and five-year-old discovered that stories from books were not enough for them. One stressful day, his imagination produced a stern schoolmarm. With creative desperation he made up the first of many tales about her. Mrs. Crabapple read moralistic stories in a stern nasal voice. She insisted there was only one right way to do things. Over several months she was at the center of spontaneous tales he told, causing outbursts of silliness and much new perspective. She became so much a real part of the household that, one day, when parents and children were at odds with one another, all of them wanting their own way, the father shouted: 'We are acting just like Mrs. Crabapple!' He sent her out of the room and they all felt amazingly better.

The same family gradually invited several other imaginary storytellers into their house. 'The children have their favorite ones, who are not necessarily the same as mine,' said the mother. 'They especially ask for the storyteller who lives in a white tent and wears polka-dotted socks. She is easy for me to imagine too and gives me lots of energetic stories. When it is time for a story the children often say: "Please call on the Lady with the Polka Dots". Intentionally changing her energy to match the children's, this inventive mother will say: 'Here, this is the story she told.' Sometimes the story is one they already know and love, to which the fun-loving story lady in the tent may add her unexpectedly colorful flourishes.

Another favorite storytelling companion of this rural family is Mr.Gleek, who brings fix-it stories from a big city. When the children want to hear about his activities, they call him on their imaginary telephone: 1-2-3-4-5 is his number. 'He has such a different personality from anyone in the family, with his cigars and heavy accent. He tells stories about his sister who chews gum, and about repairing leaky pipes and old doors,' explained the mother. Both parents tell stories about him, often finding themselves as surprised and amused by his behavior as their children are.

Many parents complain: 'I can't weave a complete story out of myself! I can't trust my imagination! I can't tell a real story without a book in front of me!' Yet children thrive on wholeness and freshness. The essential ingredients for storytelling are the same that children need for their healthy development. We may feel surprised to find ourselves enlivened and cared for as much as they are as we create and tell stories with them.

It can be a profound experience to imagine a very experienced storyteller, from another culture and time, who is linked with the first storytellers and can sing and speak in tune with the universe. Find or create a shawl or blanket for this ancient, capable storytelling part of yourself. Create a space for storytelling with a coverlet or two draped over a few chairs or a tabletop, or pinned to a corner wall. Light a little candle or lantern with the children and enjoy the womb-like interior hush, out of which great stories are born.

Creating Silence

Although children love to make a great commotion, they also long for quietness. As the decibels produced in billions of houses rise, everyone needs more silence. The hullabaloo of daily events is a constant challenge to an ear that listens: we miss the quietness of trees and of most living things. Yet allowing this quietness to reign in

17

our lives today requires ingenuity. Silence unites all the faculties of the child. It embraces thinking, feeling and willing; allows expectations to flourish; minds to open; stomachs to relax. Silence is the kindest, and the most powerful starting point for stories. Creating silence is different from waiting for children to be quiet. It is an active, radiant power. In the atmosphere of silence our hearts center into gentle rhythms, our senses open, the very pores of our skin relax.

To create silence is to strengthen a child's patient, active attention, which is the foundation for all learning. There are many ways to ease into its power. A grandmother knitted a shawl for herself from every color of the rainbow. She wanted to bring others into the peaceful radiance she experienced as, enfolded softly in the shawl, she shared stories with her grandchildren. Over many months she knitted storytelling shawls of rainbow colors and gave them to her family and friends as gifts, wrapping them around her favorite storybooks.

A middle-aged mother, exhausted every day by her two small, active sons, was also grateful to experience the gifts of silence through her own storytelling. In the busy, ambitious American suburb where they lived, she decided one day to buy an old spinning wheel. Soon afterwards she and her husband took the brave step of fencing off part of their garden and buying a quiet sheep. Over many weeks the family learned together to care for the sheep and her lambs and to card wool. As the boys' mother practiced spinning, especially at bed-time, the gentle whirr of the wheel lent an atmosphere of peaceful focus. Her fingers grew increasingly adept at spinning long strands. One evening, as the boys watched the fibers moving through her fingers, she began to 'yarn' for them a story about two lively shepherd boys. To her amazement, they loved this story and eagerly awaited a new installment. The next evening she picked up the same thread. The children helped her, through their devoted interest and satisfaction in this on-going yarn, and subsequently her husband also, to develop lively confidence in themselves as storytellers.

The quiet rhythms of our breathing immediately reach children, and the child within all of us. As we settle down to tell a child a story and prepare to say the opening words, each complete breath is heaven to children. It stimulates their own harmonious breathing. Then they can relax and give us their undivided attention from top to toe. A person who is wholly there for them inspires their confidence that the story will make them feel good and whole. Children need the quiet, creative warmth and closeness of adults. Anything less weakens their attention and leaves a hunger for relationship. The essential expectation of every child to be nourished by their parents' breathing and speech never dies. The inner call for a warm, breathing story told just for us persists until the very end of all of our lives. No quantity of books, television, tape recordings or computerized stories can fully satisfy our deepest needs for connection.

One rainy evening a mother took her children to hear a well-known storyteller. A large, rowdy crowd of children and their harried parents had filled the room to capacity. Overwhelmed by the different ages and moods of the children, the storyteller forgot to bring silence to the room before he began. The more tricks of the trade he tried, the more conflict and confusion filled the room. 'I could better have stayed home and trusted myself to have a good evening with my children,' said Katrina. 'I forgot how much I enjoy being their storyteller, how satisfying it is for them and for me.' Eventually she wrote a book about her determination to enjoy peaceful and creative time at home with her two boys.

Another mother, who was beginning to tell stories to her children, often found herself preoccupied at their bedtime. Reluctantly she agreed to let her children watch television, although she knew they would be filled with images from programs and advertisements. Other members of her storytelling circle commiserated when she told them that her children fell asleep later than usual and that they had wakened several times during the night with restless dreams. She resolved to keep their story time sacrosanct, no matter how important were her other concerns, as she knew it did her good too.

When I was sharing stories every day with children as a kindergarten teacher, I would first sit quietly in a rocking chair, listening for a few moments to my breathing. The children were soon listening too. The rhythm of my breathing and quiet rocking focused their attention more than my words. This was a great discovery for me. No matter how rambunctious they had been, they would calm down. Together our breath and pulse would deepen. As we created a balanced, peaceful enclosure, like the knitting grandmother and the spinning mother, my self-doubts and anxieties would disappear. The warmth weaving between us often allowed the words of my stories to come with surprising inspiration.

In a busy and happy kindergarten that I visit, a large soft chair sits invitingly at one end of the room. Peeking out from under its skirt is a pair of old-fashioned pointed boots, with golden laces. A large shawl is draped over its shoulders. Tucked in around its cushions are numerous small dolls, colored cloths and stones, and a hand-knit ball. When a child is in need of quiet time, has been injured, or is in need of more nurturing than the teachers can offer at the moment, the words 'Go sit in the Mother's lap' are spoken gently. This the children do willingly, curling up, leaning into the depths of the chair for succor and a quiet space alone. According to the regular ritual of the classroom, when it is time for the children to hear the story of the day, their teacher seats herself ceremoniously in this quite archetypal chair. She takes time to make herself comfortable in 'the Mother's lap' before she begins. The little dolls, stones, cloths and other items tucked into the chair sometimes come into her story. As the children develop their imagination of a wise, comforting, and accomplished 'story mother', they learn gradually to draw from her seat consoling and strengthening quietness through the stories she tells.

Many opportunities can be found to bring about more silence in the life of your family. Some parents find it helpful to place an old-fashioned clock in or near a child's room. When I was small, the big clock that stood in our stairwell with its steady beats spoke to me, though I did not as yet understand its purpose. My brothers and I loved to listen to the round disc of the pendulum pulse and bong every quarter hour. Careful listening to different kinds of sounds prepares for lively listening at story time: an evening breeze, the sound of a kitten's footsteps, your own breathing and your child's, your shifting movements, the soft rhythmic pulse of inner circulations.

A young father, a raconteur who is rarely at a loss for words, discovered the power of silence while creating a story about Indians. At first, quiet breathing and listening was strangely disquieting for him, yet recently he shared with me a story he made up at a summer evening's fire. The main character, a mysterious Indian woman, was neither deaf nor dumb, but she chose not to speak. It was as if sounds passed through her and went to a place of beautiful expectancy. Sometimes when she came to an evening campground not even the fire made a noise. In the silence around her, the people she visited in different encampments were filled with wonderful questions; when the children awoke after her visits they remembered beautiful songs from their dreams. As their father made up various stories about these Indian villages, the children often asked: 'Is the Quiet Woman coming?' Along with their father, they loved to hear about her power.

In a similar mood, during their vacation on a lake a family decided to pursue the sounds of silence. At first they could only keep quiet and listen for a few moments. They encouraged one another to listen to the spaces between their words. Finally they were able to live in quiet awareness for almost a whole day, hearing surprising music in the natural world around them. As silence for them increased they became more peaceful as a family, their gestures more eloquent. When their three-day experiment ended, one of the children wanted to continue it for the entire vacation.

What rewards come to you and your children as you take time to listen for rich, diversely breathing silences in your everyday experiences? Everything that is breathes. To nurture inner quietness in a story you create you might include the leafy song of a tree, the sigh of a boulder as the sun shines on its back, the sweet exhalation of a rose. Or a story about a country child who goes forth to listen for the breathing of everything it sees - a woodcutter, a cow, a bee.

Storytelling Awakens Listening

The power to be silent awakens dormant forces of listening and understanding. A mother made a doll especially to help her tell stories to her young children. When her small daughters were getting up from their naps, she would wake the doll very tenderly in her arms and ask: 'Would Mimi like to hear a story?' Like the children, the doll would eagerly nod her head, sometimes interrupt, or hide and cover her ears in the folds of the mother's garments. The doll helped both the children and their mother to experience different listening moods: when the doll begged for another story, the children would say: 'I wish she would learn that she can't hear stories all the time!' Mimi especially liked to whisper a question shyly in the mother's ear. 'What do you think Mimi wants to know?' the mother asked her daughters. After a while the children became adept at speaking for the doll. At the end of a story the mother created a routine: Mimi would sigh with contentment and thank the story, the storyteller and also the children for listening with her. When story and prayers were done at bedtime, a yawning Mimi, who had been listening along with the children, would go dreamily into her cradle at the children's bedside.

Different children – different stories

In both children and adults the power of listening can waken and develop to extend into those ancient storytelling parts of us that are ever attuned to moods, languages and people. Because children listen to life inside and around them in so many different ways, I like to look at their ears before I tell a story. Old shells formed in cosmic seas, each pair of ears is unique. Their individual shape and color invite words tuned in different ways. Over my years of practice with storytelling, I have learned that listeners with fiery-colored little ears especially require lively action in stories. Burning with curiosity as to what comes next, they balk when a story moves slowly. Delicately curving, graceful ears, in contrast, seek to take in light-hearted words. Perhaps not hearing every word, they receive stories easily, enjoying lilting details. Plumper ears, hungry for whatever is full and round, seem slowly to eat the dreamscape of a story. They like repetition and words that meander slowly. Cool and sensitive melancholic ears, with unique inwardness, listen thoughtfully for distress and suffering in a story, attuning to mournful tone and themes.

Children naturally draw forth from their elders different kinds of stories to meet their different moods and energy of listening. Because of differences of temperament and personality, some children prefer telling and listening to highly imaginative tales; others gravitate to practical down-to earth stories. Still others prefer stories that especially excite feelings and portray emotional truth. I recently met a sensitive grandmother who loved to read and tell fairy tales. She was bewildered by her young grandson's taste in stories. Although her own children had listened contentedly to all sorts of fairy tales when they were young, at seven years old her grandson claimed that stories about princes and strawberries in the snow were silly. He wanted straightforward stories about animals and people doing good work. He hated rabbits that had been given human characteristics and would become wildly upset if a donkey talked. Now, as a teenager, he is a practical repair-man, who happily spends long hours tinkering with cars.

I loved reading stories to my brothers and myself when I was a child. One day, when I was eight years old, an Afro-American girl, who was slightly older than I, visited our neighborhood. We children gathered around her awestruck as, arms akimbo, she sang and told a wildly imaginative story. This wondrous event gave me the idea that I too might look out into mysterious realms, sing loudly and tell stories. So one evening soon afterwards, as my six-year-old brother and I settled down before sleep, I asked if he would like to hear a story. I hoped he might like a wildly imaginative one. Instead he wanted a story about a little red truck. Although I did not like playing with trucks, I dearly loved my little brother and my imagination pictured a good truck. My brother wanted the truck to visit very real places. He wanted a story to help him grow. Today he is a very accomplished builder, with many trucks helping him in his work.

A five-year-old, evidently with a different set of goals for her future, insisted on being part of a circle of adults who were studying fairy tales in a candle-lit room. We were taking turns telling original stories based on well-loved plots: *Briar Rose, Snow White, Iron John* and others. Her mother cradled her on her lap past her usual bedtime in the candle-lit room with us, believing she would soon be asleep. During one of these evening gatherings, the child sat up suddenly in her mother's lap, announcing she too had a story to tell. With her relaxed, yet absorbed attention she had been observing how we allowed stories to move through us freely. That evening she held us spell-bound with the exquisite language and archetypal plot line of her story. As it ended, she sighed happily, curled closer to her mother and fell deeply asleep. We sat stunned and speechless at the depth to which this tender child had joined her listening with ours. She had demonstrated for us how to tell a story without being distracted by fears, self-doubts or competitive ambitions. The story itself had brought with it for her, and for us all, sublime satisfaction. Because the group had grown increasing humble in the presence of great fairytales, fortunately, no one's compliment burdened her as she finished her own reflection of them, such as 'What a clever little storyteller you are becoming,' or 'You're a better storyteller than I am.'

It is natural for children and even babies to respond to a positive story atmosphere. I have often seen wild birds, family pets, squirrels, and seals come as close as they can to a good story. It can be a pleasure to listen to yourself speaking a story, as a child would, wide open. The listening child in all adults needs to be nourished by language, image and gesture; a well-nourished child becomes a more complete adult. Listening with deep attention is an essential theme of many of the greatest fairy tales. *The Queen Bee,* a venerable old story included in the Brothers Grimm collection, shows that noble love between man and woman is only possible when there is deep, respectful listening. The hero of the story is able to disenchant a castle and awaken true love because he has heeded the voices of bees, ants, and ducks. *The Donkey* portrays a child who is determined, against great odds, to sing and play a musical instrument - in the end, because of his music, he realizes true love. The imagination at work in such stories nurtures our listening spirit, leading us toward more complete realizations of who we are and can become.

Were you one of the lucky children who were read to in your early childhood? What book or story told from memory made a strong positive or negative impression on you in your early childhood?

The highly individual way you listened depended on your personality and temperament. How is your personality and temperament different from your child's? How the same? What types of stories might your child resonate with, now and in future years?

When children's listening becomes calmly universal, the story has reached a very deep part of their inner life. Was there a story that moved you very deeply as a young child? Tell that story to your own child or grandchild. As your children tell stories, your listening helps them find words to match their imaginations. To avoid situations where they might receive flattering compliments to cause them unnecessary self-consciousness, a graceful tact is to focus on the stories themselves: their words, images, characters, and your eagerness to know what happens next.

Rhythmic Story Weaving

Rhythm is a necessity of childhood. Regular meals create a peaceful atmosphere for children to receive nourishment, to digest, and to steady their appetites; regular story times create a loving atmosphere in which to grow; regular sleep and rising times help young bodies to flourish. Physical, emotional and mental growth all develop in similarly complex patterns. Once we have attained physical maturity, we easily can forget how prolonged and complicated is the process of creating a well-balanced 'house' in which to live.

Everyone benefits from rhythmic routines: adults need a warmly rhythmic environment for sharing the events of the day and discoveries of the heart almost as much as little children do, especially in our present world. No one ever outgrows the need for satisfying verbal nourishment. The search for it can turn into a lifetime struggle for expression and for emotional security. When not satisfied at home by the primary guardians of our childhood, the need can turn into a lifetime of puzzled foraging.

Even if steady warmth and safety for storytelling was not created for you in your own childhood, nevertheless you can create it with your children. A three-year-old girl was wearing out books, and her mother, by her incessant demand for stories – in the car, during meals, even on the toilet. After her mother joined a storytelling circle, she realized that she herself was erratic in many areas of her life, eating all day long, rarely sitting down. Believing that her child's babble was more charming, important, and deserving of attention than her own, her conversations with adults became increasingly unsatisfying. She complained about this with the circle of parents who were cultivating the art of storytelling for their children. Astonished to realize that she had been unconsciously imitating her child's chaotic energy and speech, she resolved to bring more adult self-respect to all the words she spoke, both for her own sake and for her child's. She began to temper the stories she told, telling each often and well. She soon discovered how soothing and enjoyable it was for them both when she gave up the book and trusted the words to memory: seeing her mother's whole face in front of her calmed the child. They learned little nursery rhymes and rhythmic tales, repeating them regularly before meals and at bedtime every day. Soon they were developing some of them into songs and humorous games, or drawing and painting a delightful stream of pictures, and were never bored. Her child's words began to grow less chaotic and rambling. She and her daughter could look into one another's eyes with joy and delight, and join their hands and voices.

A bewildered man, a very successful entrepreneur who fathered a daughter late in life, recently told me that he had consulted a doctor because, at three years old, his child wanted everything repeated over and over again. He was incredulous - and relieved - to learn that this is normal for young children everywhere.

Instinctive knowledge of the rhythmic patterns that sustain children has broken down in recent years, and as a result many adults today rely increasingly on electronic assistance – videos, tape recorders, computerized stories – which can repeat indefinitely. Yet children in the sway of even the most excellent television programming as their primary source of rhythm, do not satisfy many of their most fundamental needs.

When a child discovers that you are reliably and thoroughly present as a storyteller, the nervous, dissatisfied need for more and more stories calms down. A long day with children can sometimes leave us stressed and tired, yet as storytellers we can find rhythmic patterns that give a reassuring sense of measure and coherence. Children of all ages build their inner life as they connect with stories' orderly structure and content. The very youngest children prefer stories that are thoroughly rhythmic in word-sounds and structure. A diet of these reliably rhythmic stories helps them build a foundation for healthy, self-regulating adult life.

Until recent times, great stories were sung in metric verse. Today there are many story collections from which to learn the pleasures of singing, clapping, and word-romping for both children and adults. Rhythmic phrases and little story chants stimulate, strengthen and open heart and soul, like sacred mantra. Before I had encountered chanting in Western and Eastern traditions, I spoke and sang nursery rhymes regularly with a group of four- to six-year-old children. Our joy and delight increased with each repetition. As we slowed down our words and gestures, our concentration and voices deepened. Gradually speeding up, the words whirled brighter until, with the last sound and syllable, they would flower like fireworks in the air around us. In this simple, sublime atmosphere many problems of the children, as well as my own, disappeared. The pleasure of sharing rhyming stories with children is a reminder that great cultures have developed spirit and maintained their languages and many of their traditional stories through the communal art of chanting.

Like rhythmic lines, rhyming words also support our need for rhythmic order and satisfy our ears' need for expectation and closure. Words that sound almost the same, chiming and echoing through a nursery rhyme or story, encourage listening and language development. Many old nursery rhymes are little tales. *Going to London* on mommy's or daddy's knee is the beginning of high adventure. *This Little Piggy Goes to Market* begins the discovery that characters, like toes, are connected within the same plot. Well-spoken rhythmic stories vitalize the child: rhymes and rhythms encourage the tremendous cumulative task of building their own bodies. Recurring rhythm sways their circulatory systems towards greater life. Rhyme may encourage bones, sinews and connective tissue to grow. Rolling and pulsing word repetition gives a sense of orderly progression – the sense of being safely embedded in a whole, nurturing context.

Finding regular times

Many families find pleasure in creating a regular story time every evening before bed, and at other special times. Even when children can read very well to themselves this island of sharing creates a steady heart-beat for the whole family. A father who wanted to create a Sunday morning story time complained that his three children, ranging in age from three to seven, would not come when he summoned them or sit still enough to hear what he wanted to say. Yet when he became thoroughly convinced of the importance of this time for them all, a new authority came into his voice and presence. He was deeply moved when his children began to look forward to the stories he wanted to share with them, and to the flowing strength of his voice.

Telling it again – and again!

Because all young children need stories regularly repeated, storytelling with them can develop saintly patience in the teller. Sometimes it can take weeks, even months until that mysterious moment when a child is satisfied and ready to move on to a new story. A mother once told me that through storytelling with her son she had developed tenacity beyond her wildest expectations. She told *The Three Billy Goats Gruff* to her son for the first time when he was four years old. Sometimes he requested it every day, then would let it go for a time. It became a ritual for them. This wise mother said that ultimately she surrendered to his need, believing that the story was helping him to prepare for events in his adult life. Twelve years later, after countless repetitions, when he was sixteen years old, he had still not entirely lost his need to hear her bring the goats safely over the troll's bridge.

A busy young mother felt humbly grateful for her own mother's patient storytelling with her four-year-old daughter. Said the grandmother: 'I am getting to the truth of the stories again and again. They can be repeated 5000 times, like an orchard full of apples.' The ring of wisdom and authority in her voice feeds her grandchild. Every child's soul needs to build strength, stability and security. Like milk, parental storytelling is a necessity. Your presence and voice and sureness of speech help them to discover theirs. Every rhyme and tale repeated with attention to each word warms the child's loving response to language.

Just as digestion and assimilation improve with a steady meal schedule, so do stories when they are part of the day's rhythm. If you make a storytelling schedule for your family for evenings and special times, such as holidays and birthdays, children will look forward to these regular story times which help them build a sense of security and confidence. You are telling for their future selves as well as their present.

Animals, humans, and plants share rhythms together. Our primary pulses move in a steady beat. Poems and stories which hold and express this rhythmic music are the natural food of growing children.

Birds in the air –

Stones on the land –

Fishes in the water –

I'm in God's hand…

Or

One misty, moisty morning

when cloudy was the weather

I chanced to meet an old man

clothed all in leather.

Fundamental rhythms also pulse through the folk music of many lands. As little children hear outside them what they are subtly experiencing in their own bodies, they feel secure and happy. Many fairy tales express a three-four rhythm. Joyous, healthy breathing rises naturally out of such well-balanced stories. In *Goldilocks and the Three Bears,* three meet a fourth character. In *The Three Billy Goats Gruff,* the troll is the fourth. In *The Three Little Pigs,* the villain sizzling in the fire comprises the fourth beat, stimulating a new round of the story. When children call for such stories and rhymes again and again, they are experiencing the vital music of their own pulses. They drink in the words and rhythm we manage to co-ordinate, and emulate us as best they can. As we patiently retell exactly the same stories for them they experience us as magically trustworthy adults. In *Vasilisa the Beautiful,* a well-known Russian fairy tale, certain words are repeated many times as Vasilisa and her mother commune through a magical doll.

Young children especially require whole stories: during a story everything else can wait. Undivided story time helps them build integrity in all areas of their lives. Who would give a child a puzzle with missing pieces or a broken ball? A circle encompasses all directions and gives a sense of enclosure and safety: together you can blow an imaginary bubble and sit together in its roundness

Voices: Spinning Gold

Where does speech originate? The holy origins of speech, although largely forgotten in the daily hullabaloo, can be found when we slow down enough to give peaceful attention to the sounds we make, and to the space and breath around our words. Your parental voice can provide a haven, especially at story time. Listening well to your own voice helps children to listen to themselves and others: your listening builds theirs. Gradually they will be able to realize the effect of words upon themselves and others. Recently, I listened gratefully to a harried mother who consciously expressed love in her voice. I was glad for her that she had discovered how to bring this warmth into what she said, like a sheltering embrace, even when she was irritated with her child. As we take increasing responsibility toward the quality and quantity of our words, a child will reflect a positive caring attitude back to us.

It is an interesting experience simply to listen to one's own voice. Speech is a combination of breath, thoughts and feelings; it arises from a subtle and complex coordination of bones, muscles and circulation. Tones conveying warmth and happiness nourish a sense of confidence. Critical tones darken the atmosphere. We can gradually come to see the weather we create with our voices. Children are at the mercy of the way we speak – our impulsive little words and the feeling tones that surround them. These root deeply and from them our words return to us again, for better or for worse. How we speak to impressionable children is likely to affect them for the rest of their lives. The feeling atmosphere of our words can shrivel or bless them. With even a little effort, we can will ourselves to shed self-criticism, worry, distractions and ambition. Steady attention and commitment is required to speak with truth, good humor, and loving kindness. Whether parents or teachers, we can intentionally invite warmth to fill and organize us from top to toe, and seek a spiritual outlook, so that love and respect can flow from our words.

Storytelling provides opportunities to ease into the vibrant music of words. People often ask me if they need to modify their normal way of speaking in order to tell stories to children and I reply that children are our guides: the bodies of infants surely invite gentle melodies to enfold them. Soft melodic lines very gradually transform; as little bodies gain weight and substance, they invite more solidity of words and syntax that sway between music and speech. What lives within our voices is evidently what matters most to them; if a heart be merry, kind and honest, even a raucous, rusty burr can charm and nourish them. I have seen very small children listen spellbound to a succession of story songs offered gently and musically to them by parent-storytellers in very different languages: Slovenian, Japanese, German, Nigerian Igbo and English.

Independent of logical meaning, in the playful rediscovery of our voices during story time, we can recover speech patterns long forgotten, perhaps being moved to tears as we ourselves are revived by them. Words and phrases from surprising lands and other times may come to nourish us. As your mouth searches the shape of sounds you speak in the presence of children, you may learn new words and feel their resonance in different parts of your body: in bones, belly and blood. When you speak with your whole self, even your feet participate. The burst and swirl of sounds emerging from mouth or throat cause the tongue to stretch and shape itself in so many fascinating ways.

Children need clearly pronounced words that begin, continue and round off with a sense of deliciousness in the mouth and freshness in the air – like a peach. They long to love and heartily enjoy the banquet of language. It is all too easy to correct, ignore or imitate children's attempts at words. A story that contains the words and phrases they want to speak gives them a gentle opportunity to listen and learn from your own speech. Rather than correcting them immediately when they mispronounce or misuse a word, at story time you can include what you hear them trying to articulate.

The instrument of the voice

A mother with a thin, nasal voice complained that she had difficulty gathering her children to hear her read stories. She said she could not hold their interest, no matter what she was saying, and feared she would never be able to change her voice. A group of parents who had gathered to practice the art of storytelling made up a whimsical story for her. It began: *Once there was a flower that wanted to roar...* Their story deeply touched her imagination, and helped her to speak more powerfully. She was surprised to discover that, when she gave herself permission to breathe deeply and play with words and expression, her children started to play with their own voices. Soon, to her great relief and surprise, as they all played more freely, her children gathered eagerly to hear her tales.

Another mother, who was bi-lingual, discovered she could move gracefully between two languages as she told her stories. This enhanced the learning of her young children. She made up and practiced several stories which united both languages. Soon she found that she could tell episodes in either language, the children attending happily to the subtle changes in her voice and words.

When they are old enough to enjoy taking roles and changing their voices, children are happy that we can do this too. They also listen for our clear, reliable, everyday voice. As they experiment and grow in expression, your uniquely loving voice is their most important stimulus for learning to integrate themselves and to counter the discordant voices they are bound to hear in the world around them. The clarity, warmth and sincerity of the stories you tell, help them develop these qualities in themselves. You also can regulate the volume of your speaking. Your voice is a subtle instrument which attunes your child to both inner and outer realities. A loud voice is not necessarily more powerful or effective.

A gentle whisper can sometimes fill a large room and hold the attention of a crowd.

Clearly formed words, phrases and sentences in poems and stories expand and enrich all of our senses. They help us listen for crops growing, winds singing, the hearts of trees. The bridge to things and people, to the truth of feelings and emotions and to all inner life, speech awakens children for spiritual life. Together with all human beings, you and your child are on an endless path of discovery of the relationship between reality and the structure and sounding of words.

Stories that portray the power of words increase respect for the human voice. Examples are *Sweet Porridge* from the Grimms' collection; the English tale *Tom Tit Tot;* the Russian fairytale *Vasilisa the Beautiful.*

In how many ways can one say: 'Once there flowed a peaceful river'? As you repeat the words, change your thoughts and notice how this affects your voice, body, and feelings. For example, behind the words you might carry a skeptical attitude or a scientific, political or poetic one. Say a phrase while standing, sitting and lying in different postures to notice how your body affects the quality of your voice.

Afterwards

At the end of a good story, a bout of clapping can be jarring and prematurely break its spell I often like to show my genuine feelings through quiet gestures. I sometimes give a big sigh of contentment and place my hands over my heart in pleasure and gratitude to show children how to open their arms wide to embrace the whole story.

Having made a special effort to prepare and to tell a story, storytellers typically feel both elation and depression. One new storyteller observed: 'Especially after an important story, I like to be still. I feel warmth in my heart. I've connected to the children through the story; I feel an opportunity for us to be held in this openness for a while before returning to the usual physical world...' A grandmother described how she lets herself feel a little tired after a session of storytelling. 'The time after a story is a rest before a new breath. Like the quiet before a new day, it can bring a sense of holiness and wholeness. Like the children at bedtime, I curl into a little cocoon. Or maybe I read a really good book, or do some heavy housework to bring myself thoroughly back into my body.'

To honor such soul-sensitive times, a large candle can be used for a whole year of storytelling. After the story has finished, to slowly come out of its spell you can carefully blow out the flame, or use a candle snuffer ceremoniously, watching the curling smoke rise. Then carefully take off your story shawl or hat, get up and move on with cheerful deliberation to another activity – washing dishes or polishing shoes. You are a role model, teaching your child how to move in and out of different states of awareness with conscious intention. From you your child learns to bridge wisely and gracefully between different worlds.

Stories often come from beyond the person who has been speaking them. Says a puppeteer friend: 'A good story is golden light flowing through a little sky in the back of my mind. It doesn't stop with the children. I feel the sharing of the story gives its Source great joy, just as it does to myself and the children. A berry catches it; a bird eats the berry.'

When children question a story, they are not necessarily asking for explanations and interpretations. Instead of answering directly, it is often preferable to simply echo the whole or a portion of a story. You can ask them respectfully to find the answer to their own question. Interpretive logic is a mental ability that blooms best in later years. Adult reflection on meaning can detract from the more fundamental nourishment of word and image. A story left intact is likely to have a healthy life of its own in dreams, emerge in play and become part of the household for a short or a long time. Yet even a quite simple, harmless story, whether it has been read or told, can be disturbing to a child or their parent. 'I'm sorry this story frightened you,' or 'Tell me what you didn't like in the story' can increase the discomfort. If a story you have read or told upsets you or your child, you can erase it decisively with: 'When you are a little older this story will be just right,' or 'Well, that story is certainly not for me!' Children will usually identify happily with you. When my mother disapproved of a story she would say with an imperious gesture, 'Phewy on that!'

A father recently told me that, although he usually only read stories he already knew to his seven-year-old, he was appalled to find that every character at the end of a lavishly illustrated tale, both good and bad, had met a terrible end. 'I felt helpless,' he said. A member of the storytelling circle suggested he might have said: 'Let's send that story to God for improvement.'

Yet a difficult story may be the very one that a child needs; growth can be uncomfortable. Adult distaste for stories can sometimes cramp a child's freedom. When in doubt about whether or not a story was good for your child, you can safeguard even a terrifying tale, and also shield your child's right to freedom of imagination, giving them a sense of solidarity with other children, by saying:

'This is a very old fairy tale from long ago, that has been heard by many children through the ages and is still heard today.'

Your own openness also helps to nudge difficult stories toward corresponding aspects of children's inner lives. As you tell such a story with steadfast kindness in your heart, your presence supports children's ability to absorb the deeper messages of the story, and stimulates their wide and heartfelt reading later on.

2 The Storyteller's Trove of Treasure : Memory and Imagination

Love every ray of light; love the animals;
Love the plants; love every leaf, love each separate thing.
Fyodor Dostoyevsky

Happiest are those who are able to trace an unbroken connection between
the end of life and the beginning.
Johann Wolfgang von Goethe

Memory

The story of what happened today

'Tell me again what happened today,' squeals a four year old with delight. He gathers himself together to study what his parents notice, remember, and say about his experiences and feelings: his waking up, his broken shoelace, his hungry pet. The natural desire of children to review with a kind attentive adult the details of their day, helps them prepare for sound sleep. Hearing us speak about their accomplishments, feelings and discoveries, they weave their experiences into a nest of understanding and dreams.

As a storyteller, you can help your children round out their day and make sense of it as a whole. Every day is structured like a story with a beginning, middle, and ending. From you, your children learn how to love their reality and to organize it into language. As you put their experiences warmly into words for them, gradually they develop a sense of personal time and memory and learn to perceive the feelings of others almost as their own. 'You sang to the birds before breakfast.' 'Grandpa laughed till his belly shook.' 'We heard the postman whistling today.' As children hear the events in the lives of others spoken of with as much love, delight and respect as their own, they develop a lively rapport with whatever comes their way. A mother recently told me she has kept a large and lovely shell at her daughter's bedside since she was very young; often before sleep she lights a candle and puts the shell to her ear to hear news of their day.

Even before they are one year old, children can begin to respond to tales about the things and activities of their day as they are learning to walk and talk. Sharing, receiving and giving, desire and satisfaction - all the objects around them, their moods and

activities, seek words. As you join your voice lovingly to their experiences, your words playing in and around them can stimulate delight in language that will persist into their adult years. Boundlessly absorbing what is around them as they awake from naps or at the end of their day, they are especially open to the feel and lilt of words. Little dramatic moments of their day make the best stories. Deep instincts and intuitions guide us to know what they need to hear,

Although hesitant at first, a mother decided to let herself make time for a daily routine at the end of the day with Sarah, her three-year-old daughter. She always began in a firm and gentle voice as she blended memory and imagination: *Once there was a little girl named Sarah Elizabeth. She lived in a big brown house with her mother, her father and her dog. Her friend Sarah Mouse lived in a little hole in the kitchen wall.* These stories reflected on the child's daily experiences, her pleasures and questions, her upsets and fears. Often Sarah Mouse would have adventures parallel with young Sarah's. The little mouse had relatives, friends and foes who lived in bush, briar and forest.

Evening stories to review the day can build rapport between siblings. Often tired at the end of the day, a father discovered that he gained much delightful energy by giving his undivided attention to reviewing the day with his sons. The protagonists in his on-going stories were exactly their age; their names were the middle names of the real boys. They lived with their parents and two big guard dogs with golden eyes. The father reliably began each ongoing adventure: *Once there were two little boys, who lived in a house by the side of the road with their mother and their father, and two good dogs.* When the boys were very young, the adventures of the boys in the story were just like the lives the real boys had that day, including the weather and their various moods and activities. As the children became older, the dogs became more magical.

A particularly chaotic day with children can be transformed through a tale about an orderly family in which the parents are grateful for a beautiful day; and the children play happily together and brush their teeth before their prayers. A weather-loving mother created stories which always began with two children waking up to look out the window at the changing sky. After getting dressed and eating a good breakfast, the children in her stories went to visit people, pets, gardens and shops. Their journeys sometimes became increasingly imaginative as the children reached six and seven, yet each time the protagonists returned safely home to supper and sleep.

Aware of the children's need for a story at the end of the day, many adults today turn on videos, tape recorders, computerized stories, and other such entertainment. Yet a unique story which comes from an adult who knows the true, immediate daily life of the children provides a very different experience for them.

As you create stories to highlight your child's experiences, include in a calm and loving voice their happiness, distress and questions. Each story will offer you both reassurance and reflection at the end of the day, especially when you speak with even-toned loving care. Children readily fill in missing details that are important to them.

Bringing your personal memories to life

Little children tend to experience everyone with loving acceptance in present time, in the here and now. Yet at four or five years old they begin to want to hear about you and other adults at their age. Where did you live? Who did you play with? Who and what did you love? What do your parents remember about you as a child? As you share your anecdotes with them they especially study your feelings.

Because they have an eternal sense that they, and all creation, are watched over and loved, they need to hear their whole family group spoken of with loving and positive interest. Children can learn from us to respect and empathize with other family members. A clear-thinking, spirited grandmother often stands in front of her long mirror with her grandchildren, saying: 'Thank you for every moment that I can stand here and feel how wonderful I am. My parents took care of me when I was a little girl. I am so grateful they wanted me to practice and study and sing and do all the things that make my life happy today.' Then she sits down in her favorite chair to share with them stories about her life as a small child: having meals, working and playing, the struggles between her mother and father, between herself and others. She tells them how she and her seven brothers and sisters loved having new shoes, where she lived and how she and the other children in her family received their names. She groups her favorite childhood memories in natural categories: by days of the week, months, seasons and years. 'When I was four years old in June I would watch bees in the bluebells in my grandmother's garden. My grandmother filled me with her love,' she says. 'In September I always went to school; in March my brothers tapped the maple trees for sweet sap; on Saturdays I woke up with the sun and rushed outside.'

A mother whose children were teenagers wanted to prepare herself to be a grandmother who could speak wisely and well about her family history. By trial and error she unlocked her imagination, creating the beginning of a story for herself that rang true to her real life:

Once there was a princess who inherited a treasure house from her ancestors. When she grew old enough to know that the treasure house was there and that it was hers, she went to the door and asked to see what was inside. But there were two officers guarding the door. One of them said: 'The things in this house are very old. They are no good anymore.' The princess begged to be allowed to see and decide for herself but the two officers crossed their spears and she could not pass. So the princess went out into the world and became wise but she always wondered about the treasure house of her ancestors. When her children had almost grown up and her hair had begun to turn gray she journeyed once more to the door of the treasure house. There were new guards at the door with clear and compassionate eyes.

Although your own early childhood may seem to be lost in a gray cloud, and your memories are sparse, children nonetheless need to know that you can remember yourself as a child with respect and

kindness. Even the cruelest of childhoods, can be turned into compassionate insightful tales.

Whatever parenting you received, it is your birthright to be a family storyteller today and to take good care of family lore. About a personal tale you can ask: How is this a love gift for my children? How will it help them to grow in qualities I admire: strength, kindness, courage, loyalty, happiness, humor? A friend of mine tells this story about herself:

My father was working in the garden. I took some little sunflower seeds out of the bird feeder and went behind the pine trees. I planted all of them. I dug little holes with my fingers. I borrowed Daddy's big watering can and carried it, walking barefoot on soft warm sticky pine needles, to my little garden. The seeds grew. I kept telling my mother about my little garden but she didn't believe me. So one day I begged and pleaded for her to come to see it. She couldn't believe her eyes. My sunflowers had grown even taller than she was.

Our early memories can provide the foundation for multitudes of little anecdotal tales. These memories often have been formed in connection with plants, animals and human companions who played a part in our earliest years. During a storytelling group dedicated to sharing childhood memories, a familiar willow tree swayed in the mind's eye of a busy professional who believed she had no childhood to share with her children. Encouraged to make a list of words and phrases connected with this vision, she wrote: 'Low, thick branches; yellow green golden bark; a canopy of subtle branches blowing in the wind; bumpy roots; violets.' Suddenly she remembered climbing the young willow tree in her back yard in the springtime when she was six or seven years old. There, in wonder, she had found a nest of delicate sky-blue robins' eggs, and on another day peeping babies. Soon there shimmered back to her a similar vision of the pines planted by her grandfather in her back yard, and the pain of seeing them cut down at Christmas; the faithful oak that held her swing all through her childhood; the poison-berry tree, a little fortress against the marauding teenagers in her neighborhood; the birch tree on which she leaned, her companion when she was learning to read. As her list of friendly trees from her childhood lengthened, she knew that, after all, she was well-supplied with memories to make into stories.

At around six years of age, many children also begin to want to hear about significant lessons their parents and grandparents had to learn when they were little. Did they wear shoes that did not match to school, or forget to set a place for themselves at the table? Did they cross a street without asking, and receive a punishment? Throw stones at cars? Katrina, an editor, who joined a story circle to gather confidence in telling stories spontaneously to her children and later went on to write about her story-experiences, told us about the night she and her husband first became storytellers. It was during a long ride home with her sons, then

48

aged three and six. At first they reminisced gently for the children, but soon, drawn out by their older boy, found themselves speaking 'blood and bone' memories of childhood. Her husband accidentally hit his best friend with a rock, hurt himself with an ax and was bitten by a dog. She gave dramatic accounts of the day she rode her horse into a wasps' nest and was thrown to the ground and stung in seven places; of broken bones; a full gold-fish bowl overturned on a head; and a great-great uncle's demise under a tractor wheel. In the heat of these anecdotes, she writes: 'We were home too soon. What's more, we had whetted an apparently insatiable appetite for stories.'

Compliant and considerate children can surprise their parents because of their eagerness to hear such stories. I used to visit two girls who always wanted me to tell them stories about the naughtiest children I knew. These girls were particularly good girls who longed for some extra dash in their lives. I made a lot out of a little naughtiness, knowing that children do not reason like adults and unwittingly tend to imitate. Stories abound that delight older children who are especially obedient, such as *Pippi Longstocking* and *Ronia, the Robber's Daughter* by Astrid Lindgrun.

You can safeguard your feelings and give them distance by telling your childhood memories from a surprising point of view. Many choose to tell incidents from the viewpoint of the house they lived in, or of a tree that watched over their house To young children, everything is alive with feelings: the heart of a house or garden can be happy or sad or exuberant. The perspective of an outside observer – perhaps a postman or a lively real or fictional neighbor, might also release a flow of your memories. A pleasant, playful way to dig up old bones is to speak about your childhood through a family pet. 'Once upon a time there was a dog named… who lived with a small family in a brown house on a busy street.' If critical or sarcastic family members are present as you tell a story, you can request they listen to the story *as a story*, saying that you feel quite vulnerable when you are sharing your memories with your children and need their respectful listening.

A father who was bringing up his boys while his wife worked began when they were very young to take them to many places he had been as a boy. Each of these occasions prompted stories about his life. There were joyful outings years later when his sons returned with him and their own children to some of their father's favorite places to hear the stories again. Another father who was burdened throughout his childhood by his father's silence and secrecy, often introduced his stories to his son: 'When I was a boy I had many adventures and dreams.' This confirmed his son's sense that he could dream his own independent dreams.

Family members who have behaved unconventionally can inspire a family storyteller, especially when children reach the rebellious teenage years. Then they can enjoy such psychologically vivid biographies as H.E.Bates' *My Uncle Silas* or Gerald Durrell's *My Family and Other Animals*. But young children are not ready for stark biographical details. Outstandingly sad or peculiar family members are better perceived as imaginary characters. Telling them that your grandfather was an alcoholic or your grandmother never worked a day in her life, is too judgmental and abstract.

Children look for the love and respect you have for yourself and your experiences. You may find it satisfying to remember a time in your childhood when you were creative, persistent or courageous. Choose one memory and prepare to tell this as a little story. You will find yourself nurtured by your own remembrances. Children can keep a whole story intact with impressions of your storytelling that can deeply influence their adult lives. Many parents start a notebook to collect stories from their childhood, perhaps beginning: 'When I was a little child about your age', with stories about their mother, father, sisters, brothers, the children next door, and about visits to your grandparents and other relatives or friends. Using simple words, you might tell about a favorite tree; a hiding place; a pet; a holiday; or a friend. Your own love and wonder will instill these qualities in your children.

Before the invention of the printing press memory was a much more active force. Play 'Do you remember when?' As you write out these memories and read them back as a story, allow the structure and framework to help the children remember, and to give them a feeling of the importance of cherishing memories. Try your own variation on: In a country called__ in the city of __on the street called __ where I lived when I was ___ years old...

Imagination

Spontaneous storytelling

Just when you think a story is going one way, you may experience creative currents moving it in a new direction. One mother complained: 'All the time I am telling a story I'm not sure I'm giving my daughter what she wants.' Uncertainty is creative; it asks us to pay attention with much more than our ordinary consciousness. Names of characters or places or plot line may alter unexpectedly, words nudge at our ears, or a sudden onrush of feelings surprise and unbalance us.

Spontaneously created stories can be mysterious collaborations. As a teacher, I soon noticed that the process of making a story for a child or group of children was subtle and complex. Although I often do not understand why, later events in their lives often provide an explanation for me. Sometimes I have met a grown child who has told me how much a story meant to them, and only then could I begin to appreciate what for me had been obscure. I learned to trust the images, words, thoughts and feelings that would spring between them and myself. I discovered many different elements at work at the same time - my love for the children, my desire for them to be nourished by the story, my puzzlement at what to say. By observation and questioning, I sensed that the stories often came from their higher selves or from their personal or family strengths and dilemmas. The children's need to be known and to grow was inspiring both the content and mood of the stories. Often I felt I was guided by some greater benevolent power.

My cardinal rule was to place my heart and soul and mind at the service of the children. I discovered that, along with the children's, my imagination enjoyed playing and performing helpful tasks. We saw solutions to problems, made inventions, satisfied hungers and yearnings. Fears calmed; doubts transformed. Through images evolution was happening: I saw that the inner life of the children needed protection and assistance as they created hopes and dreams, resilience and immunity. After creating many spontaneous stories, whether standing before the children or privately with pen and pencil, I became more familiar with the creative process. Fascinated and nurtured by this higher communication with them, I have shared this way of storytelling with others for many years.

Yet I am often reluctant to make up a story, just as you probably are. I have learned that resistance is part of creativity. While working with groups of parents to develop the art of spontaneous storytelling, sometimes as we harnessed our reluctance a mysterious alchemy produced words from a sacred source beyond us: enhanced imagination and beauty of expression opened us to the souls of the children. At the end of these stories we sat in wonder and gratitude for the wisdom and love that had spoken through us.

Young children cause us to reach into our deeper selves to overcome resistance to expression; they want everyone to be lively creations like themselves. Your unique creative warmth, the playful light in your eyes, everything about you is potential grist for their growth. Your unique imagination is important to your child. If you go only to published sources for stories, you are teaching your children to do the same.

Yet invariably the creating of stories invites contradictory feelings. One mother recently told me that when her son asks her to tell a story she always believes that she can't. But as soon as she starts, 'something amazing begins to happen'. Like her, every storyteller experiences a combination of knowing and ignorance, courage and fear, confidence and humility. There is no escaping from these contradictory states of mind, which are familiar to every creative person. Yet loving, devoted attention to children and to the story process can generate, as it has for countless ages, true communication with them. A father who joined a circle of storytelling parents, found an opportunity one evening to tell his first story to his little son and unexpectedly discovered many stories within him. Reflecting on this experience afterwards, he said: 'My son was completely entranced. And so was I at the whole process. When I looked into my imagination I found a shimmering stream and fished. After the first rush of images, I selected one. I stayed with it and created the story around it.' A mother who rejoined this adult storytelling circle after telling an original story to her young daughters expressed similar surprise. She reported triumphantly, 'My youngest told me I was the best storyteller in the whole world. It was the way the children listened that kept me going. Although I was not always sure whether they were enjoying it, I was so absorbed in the story that I continued to the end. It was like threading the images onto a necklace. Afterwards we were strangely full of wonder and peace. The children wanted me to repeat the story again and again. They helped me to remember it.' Both these parents had discovered a new role and one of the great pleasures of parenting. They had tapped into a profoundly benevolent wellspring of creativity.

As her child helped her to create the stories she needed to hear, another mother said with scientific glee: 'It is as if my body goes right out somehow and mixes with my daughter's – heart to heart, blood to blood. Then hers come back to me. They pass back and forth in a sort of osmotic exchange. It is strange but true.' Expressing her wonder at the same mysterious process, another said: 'We are in a well of images together. Or perhaps it is that the children need to drink from my well and I from theirs. It is difficult to know who is who sometimes, or where the pictures come from that are particular to our relationship.' Such exchanges can be surprisingly profound. A mother said of her 4-year-old adopted Oriental daughter: 'She pulls cosmic stories out of me.' When her child asked where the fish, the bird, the dog went when they died, she found herself speaking of different levels of heaven. Images came to her of guardian spirits distinctly unfamiliar to her.

A gentle and sensitive mother told me recently that when she sat down with her daughters to give them a story of her own making, she was truly frightened at first to open herself to pictures arising in her imagination. Yet each time a story finished, she said, 'I had a feeling of being helped, as if I were being guarded and guided all along by an invisible goodness.' I, also, often have this experience. Fear usually shakes my resolve when I make up a story that I hope will be in the service of a child's real needs. Yet when I focus on the child, a wise creative presence steadies me. I sense images and concerns of the child being transferred to me for expression; the imaginings often bring with them a sense of blissful wonder. 'Here. Look, this is for you!' It is something special we can share, like a goat sensing a deliciously fresh grassy patch for its kids. The story happens; like sunlight and birdsong, it speaks for itself to bring happiness and nourishment. Parents and the child belong to the story, and the story to a playful universe. The connections feel positive and safe.

When children want spontaneous stories, they are appealing to the child-like part of our psyches, which are attentive, adventuresome and full of wonder. Imaginative stories are often rooted in patterns of the human soul only slightly bound to the material world. Each image can be a small vision. Swifter than reason, even more ingenious than dreams, imagination gives us access to invisible people, places and times. It helps us survive difficult situations, showing us pictures of what to do, where to go and how to grow. As you focus with confidence on your visionary faculties and create stories, the children absorb and learn this skill from you through a unique symbiosis. A mother complained as she was learning to tell stories set free from the immediate environment: 'The thing is dissolving while I'm telling it. I want my stories to be more developed, coherent, cohesive.' Another said,' I can relate to certain images but I can't seem to string a flow. It is the same with my memories. It is as if they are bound to a snapshot, and that is it!' How can imagination be freed so that it can move in a whole harmoniously flowing pattern, that gives confidence from the outset that the story will end well?

Simple, positive suggestions, such as: 'Take a deep breath, start and keep on going until the end!' help a storyteller to experience the story as a whole before saying a word. Many of the fundamental patterns that storytellers have followed nurture the blessed optimism that belongs to childhood. They move a main character reliably through a series of tests toward a 'happily ever after' ending. The golden format includes obstacles and helpers, who may come surprisingly out of the depths and heights to help speed the journey toward safety and love. The very real obstacles we face every day, seen through the eyes of imagination, may take many forms. A father turned his daughter's temper into a hot-headed little fairy who blew out fires and made mischief wherever she went. A quick-moving father, in despair over his daughter's slowness, started an on-going story about a family of lumbering giants whose daughter wanted to move a little more quickly than her parents did. Into each of these stories, when the going was rough, help came – dancing shoes, a white rabbit, an angelic rainbow bird. I have never tired of working with the pattern that causes the main character to move, with surprising help, through impediments, to arrive mysteriously in a realm of greater life, love and happiness.

A circle of mothers gathered to understand their children and to weave stories for them. First they explored creativity and humor – the airy laughter that bursts quickly into a bibble-babble of quick, light word play. Some of them invented little two- or three-minute melancholic stories, that ingeniously transformed woe into hilarity, or a story in a fiery mood into one with sudden practical jokes or slapstick. Others made up a little slow-moving story permeated with a sense of comfort and genial laughter. Out of these experiments they eventually became aware of four fundamental moods for telling stories with their children.

Four elements

I offered them the guide-lines that have helped me to create and organize stories for many years. 'If your child is full of fire,' I said, 'stomps about the house, lets you know what he wants and doesn't want, has strong shoulders and a fighting sense of life – then you need not waste your time with a story about a little gerbil quietly waking up in the morning.' In my experience, children full of fire like to be met with a bold story whose energy meets their own. They seek a vigorous, fast-paced plot which may include hornets, impalas or red peppers.

Children who seem more connected with air than with fire, who leap lightly about on their toes seeking more height - respond to lovely lilting stories filled with bright birds and graceful flowers, smelling of sweetness and light.

By contrast, some children really enjoy a tale about the death of a bird or spider. To their parents' bewildered dismay, their interest picks up when a story is centered around fears, sorrows or wounded feelings. Melancholic brooding asks for a story in its own true dominant mood.

A more contented, phlegmatic child, however, who comfortably observes life, responds best to a story in which everyone will be well-nourished and predominantly calm throughout. Phlegmatic, slower-moving children tend to give their undivided attention if you begin a story with an extensive and delicious feast.

'But what if I can't change my own dominant mood to match my child's?' implored one mother. I shared a discovery that has proved true so many times for me: that story time is a refreshing opportunity to explore and to transform moods. ' If your child's fire is flaring,' I suggested, 'at story-time you might get out that

twelve-year-old red-feathered hat and put it on backwards. If your child is a restless prancer, try stepping into a pair of brilliant yellow shoes and toss a flower behind your ear. Or to soothe yourself to a more contented disposition, brew a quieting pot of tea; then surprise yourself and your child by wrapping up softly in a long sea-green shawl. Or if tears have been hiding for days behind your child's eyes, invite sorrow to be your storyteller and put on a moth-eaten blue babushka. Enjoy meeting all your child's moods with artistic flair, in league with the long ages of creative imagination that support all storytellers.

With four dominant temperaments in mind, each of the mothers in the group decided to create a special doll or puppet to help them tell stories to their children. These emerged during the weeks that followed: airy little elves, a red queen, a fiery-faced gnome, a sad blue story-horse. For one of these mothers it was a great experience to sew a moss-green gnome. She wanted him to be a friendly, easygoing spirit to resemble her sons, who were three- and six-years-old at the time. 'Mossy' became part of their household and a pleasantly phlegmatic and powerful helpmate in a series of remarkable stories she told them. She worked hard to write the first episode. From the effort she made, and the satisfaction of her children after she memorized and told it to them, she gained confidence to tell her stories more spontaneously. With many vivid and sensitive episodes. Believing that spiritual help came to her through Mossy, she held her little creation, her first episode began.

Once upon a time there was a little fellow named Mossy. He lived inside a hollow oak tree in the deep green forest. He had made himself a very comfortable and sheltered home in the old oak, and since he was a pleasant fellow the old oak didn't mind at all. She was very generous and shared her branches and leaves and bark with several others besides Mossy.

Mossy was not a pretty sight with his face all wrinkled, his beard wild and long. But he was good-natured and didn't have any enemies. One day Mossy was digesting breakfast on his daily walk. He loved this daily walk; it gave him the feeling that everything was in order. The hustle and bustle of others made him feel rushed and uncomfortable. But he would take a deep breath, draw inward a little, and keep going with a steady pace.

This morning, just as he reached the edge of the forest, someone barked at him from behind: 'Get out of my way, you pot-belly.' Slowly and with emphasis Mossy turned around and saw a stranger on a dark horse, short of breath. ' I am not accustomed to being addressed in such a manner,' Mossy said slowly, stressing each word. 'Get used to it,' yelled the other.

As the story continued, the old oak told the little forest gnome about Bossy, a gremlin on a nasty mission to take human boys

away from their mothers. Eventually Mossy successfully intervened, but Bossy on a black horse rudely appeared in other episodes. This mother knew she had tapped into her sons' deep fears and challenges in the neighborhood and at school, and to very significant new horizons for herself as a storytelling mother. After a while, the children knew to ask when they needed another Mossy story.

You too can create or find simple dolls to express the characteristic mood and energy of your children. Let the dolls become the central characters in a story or two. Create plot, images and language that you feel is tuned with your child.

Perhaps you might create a simple gnome doll like the mother who sewed a little green gnome-like fellow for her two small boys and named it from its natural surroundings Gnomes, custodians of gravity, hear the musical booming of the stones, the drone of rocks patiently holding their places. You might imagine a gnome finding a geode, emerald or wonderful rock. Using stones and sticks as musical instruments, imagine their songs from within mountains or along fields.

Of course, imagination also develops in relationship with books. A mother who grew up with few books of her own says her daughters inspire her to feel a warm connection with theirs. 'When I give a new book to them I choose it carefully and read it myself in advance. I make each one special.' Books are alive; especially to young children, wonders can waken from inside their covers. A story that is loved and has a life of its own shines these qualities to the child. When I tell or read a story from a book, I often say to young children that the story and the pictures have been dreaming and want to wake up and come out to play with them. A young child can make sense of this. It builds a mood of interaction with word and pictures. A Chinese infant who was adopted into an American family developed a unique relationship with each of her new parents. Her father brought home books for her from his many travels, which she kept carefully. With her mother, however, she asked to read just one book, sometimes for several weeks. She surprised her father one day when she gratefully received his gifts, but precisely requested: 'Please stop giving me so many choices.'

When children want to read at an early age, they especially need parents who are 'living books' and are willing to speak to them from the pages of their real lives. The best way to inspire your children to relate well to printed books throughout their lives may be to help them listen well to their own experiences and to yours. Says one unabashed grandmother, who alternately tells stories about herself and reads the best books she can find to her grandchildren, ' I am in this adventure of storytelling for myself. Through the stories the children inspire me to make myself more complete. I am realizing who I am right along with them. I thank God I can do this'. In another mood, a mother said firmly: 'Although my child can be enraptured to see me struggling and trying, pushing out creative energy like he can do for hours at a time, sometimes I don't have any stories to tell. My son asks me for a 'whole story' and wants to know that I am grown up and have whole stories stored up just for him. Sometimes I have to say: '*I am empty today and hungry for a story too. Let's find one together.*' Then we look at a tree, a cloud, a chair, a cat; and a simple straightforward story comes from them. Is there anything in the world that does not have a story to be told? Through wanting to satisfy my son's hunger for stories I realize now that even ordinary drinking water has come a long journey, a stone on a path has endured adventures, a pot or a pencil or a tablecloth has met with many situations and people.'

Lewis Carroll masterfully transformed the experiences of his favorite children into imaginative stories, with an unusually spiritual perspective on their inner development. In the process he also brought himself great delight. As is often true for the best stories, Carroll felt bone-tired the day he first began to create spontaneously his now world-renowned *Alice in Wonderland* adventures, which the real child, Alice, later begged him to write down for her. The narrative he eventually wrote was a profoundly playful testament to her spirit. It included songs, jokes, and games and places they enjoyed together, transformed through wit of phrase and image, a skill which he had developed with his own brothers and sisters. Frank Baum's *Wizard of Oz* series resulted from stories he told to his own children. Like Carroll, you can experiment by telling a story when you are very tired, which playfully and deeply honors your children - and notice its effect on both you and them.

3 A Storyteller's
Trove of Treasure: Play

And young and old come forth to play. . .
John Milton L'Allegro

I can whistle, I can sing, I can do most anything.
Shepherd's Hay:
Traditional English song and dance

Story Frames

Just as you gather your ingredients before you start to cook a good meal, before you tell a story you can make preparations to ensure that it will be enjoyable, satisfying. You might first straighten the room and turn down or turn off the lamp; or humming, light a candle; or sing a rousing or a soothing song. Traditional Rumanian storytellers sometimes begin playfully: 'A long time ago, when mice ran after cats…' In the Bahamas you might hear a storyteller beginning with: 'Once upon a time, a very good time, not my time, not your time, old people's time…' As they gather up their imaginative faculties I have witnessed many parents creating their own openings for storytime with their children:

Once upon a time there was a storyteller. Everyone was sitting around the fire with him. He was watching the flames dance, and in the midst of them he could see stories moving. And this was the story he told…

Or

Once upon a time there was a storyteller but when she started her story the crows came down and squawked. She said, 'Go away!' but they would not. So she said: 'Fly away,' but they would not. So she said: 'Crows, if you want to stay, be quiet.' And they were all quiet. So at last she could start her story and the people listened, and this is the story she told…

One day in a storytelling class several parents experimented opening their stories in another language important to them. Creating verses and very simple melodies, they sang in Igbo-Nigerian, Dutch, German, French, Japanese, Portugese etc. while supporting their voices with simple instruments: thumb piano,

xylophone, zither, tambourine and lyre.
Aka nni kwo aka ekpe,
Aka ekpe akwo aka nni.
When the right hand washes the left,
The left also washes the right.

de glimmende vis, ze zwemt in de zee
ze zwemt en zingt: oh kom met me mee_
The gleaming fish, she swims in the sea,
She swims and sings: O come with me...

Kleiner bunter Schmetterling,
lass mich auf Dir sitzen.
Trag mich in das Märchenland
auf Deinen Angelspitzen.
Little colorful butterfly,
Take me with you to the sky,
Carry us to fairyland —
With your wingtips I expand.

La mer, la terre, les astres là haut
Nous partageons de tout ce qui est beau.
Sea, land, stars above,
With beauty we share our love.

Ojichanga bokuni Hio okosu
tameni chodo ii okisano
When I was gazing at the night sky, suddenly
the stars started to shine more brightly together.

Pim...pi...ri...li...pim...re...
Pozinho mágico de estória
Está chegando até mim!

Peen, pe, ree, lee, peen, re…
  Magic dust of story,
  Is shining through me.

A grandfather who loved boating with his grandchildren taught them to call back to him like oarsmen when he was about to launch into a story: To his 'Let's go!' the children shouted back jubilantly, 'Pull away!' A grandmother who had been neglected as a child created a reassuring 'frame' for the stories she shared with her grandchildren –

Once there were two little girls,' she would say,' who lived at the edge of a forest. One day they decided to explore it; they wandered for a long time until at last they found a neat little house among the trees. Then they heard a friendly old voice calling: 'Come in for supper now, dears. I am expecting you.' After a good supper of _____, the old woman asked if they would like to hear a story. 'Yes, very much,' said the little girls. So the grandmother sat in a rocking chair, and this is the story she told them…

The storyteller always concluded her stories in the same way:

When the story was over the grandmother placed a cloak softly on each girl's shoulders. It seemed made just for her. Then she showed them a clear path. 'You may return here on this path whenever you need a story,' said the grandmother. Then the little girls went home contentedly to bed…

Children thrive on a peaceful and satisfying ritual to end stories. For the youngest children, singing a simple melody closes the story door gently. You too can create your own 'frame' for opening and closing stories with children.

Ways to Learn Stories by Heart

'Again! Again!' and with still more determination they insist that we tell it again. Why do young children have such rapturous enthusiasm for repetition? At our umpteenth repetition they are still studying us, testing us with scientific persistence until they are satisfied we can shape the same words in our mouths for them, arch our eyebrows to the same height, precisely wriggle our ears and chin just so. They look to us as models, as they undergo multitudes of chaotic and bewildering changes, for coordinating all aspects of their growth. From us they learn to love a story and to tell it directly out of themselves.

Of course, there are many ways to learn to tell stories for their sake.

Read the story aloud
Although some parents worry that they could never memorize a whole story, to some extent every story sings its own song and remembers itself. A mother whose children often begged her to tell stories, rather than read to them from books, finally surrendered to their need. She chose her first fairy tale because it was short. Several months later, with an extensive repertoire of stories to tell from memory, she says, 'When I want to learn a story, I imagine myself listening to it with my children. In free moments during the day or in the evenings before sleep, I read it aloud to myself all the way through, including a silent time before and after the story. After I have read it aloud to myself a number of times, it begins to feel heart and soul like an old friend. Each word breathes with a life of its own.'

Create a picture gallery of the story
Any story you want to learn from memory can be viewed like a sequence of pictures in a gallery. A father explained that for him,

getting to know a story is often very much like meditation. 'I stay with the story, sending distractions away. I dream about it. I lie on my back, call the story pictures and let them come into my mind's eye.' When you wish to tell a story as a whole, using your imagination you too can circle back through the gallery of pictures and look at every image, from ending to beginning, perhaps studying one or two pictures longer than the others. When the whole story has visually awakened within you, as you contemplate each part of it, forms, colors, and meanings will appear to you. You may want to sketch the pictures in simple diagrams; or with a palette of watercolors or pastels, paint the flow of the whole story on a large piece of paper. As you activate your own imagination, the children will also.

Create an inner theater

See the events of a story as if they are taking place in a children's theater under wise and wonderful direction. When you are relaxed before sleep, or after reading a story, imagine scenes as they might be play-acted, dwelling on details of color and gesture. After you and your children know the story, it will naturally transform into imaginative play, perhaps with dolls, puppets and costumes.

Sing the story

Singing the whole or a part of a story enchants the ears and opens the heart. Many young children sing back to themselves their own version of a story they love. The child within us likewise can sing spontaneously the whole or parts of a story. Through melody, memory of the words of a story will be activated at a deeper level. It is a fascinating fact that people who are suffering from Alzheimer's disease may not remember the names of family members but usually can sing all the songs they knew as a child.

Write the story

A venerable fairy tale or other beautifully written story inspires this kind of reverent attention and effort. Sometimes you may feel it is important to learn every word in a story exactly in place. If you enjoy your own handwriting write the story out, perhaps in a special notebook. As you slow you down and become more in touch with the shape of its words, sentences and paragraphs, you welcome the story into your personal treasury and repertoire,

Walk about

To 'remember' a story,' says one young storyteller, 'I walk! The rhythm of walking and of nature help me put a new story right into my feet.' She first jots down the 'pillars' of stories she wants to learn on a piece of paper to take with her on her walk. Another mother, who seldom is free to take a walk alone, told me that she imagines her feet on a path while she is in the process of memorizing a story. Like many a poet and storyteller, William Wordsworth used to compose poems in his head while walking through the Lake District in England.

Listen to tape recordings

Storytellers sometimes use driving time to listen to a story, perhaps recorded in their own voice, with their own turns of phrase and expression. A father who is often away from home on the open road, listens to himself reading stories on tape, accompanying himself with his own songs and guitar, until he knows every word. He is grateful to be doing something creative for his children during his long workdays on the road.

Learn to recognize story structure

Every good story has form. Sitting in a relaxed and attentive mood, breathing freely, eyes closed, invite a story to reveal its structure to you. Stories are organized in many ways.

Word music: Often children delight in the sounds of the words more than any meaning they produce. Story time for them is a word bath. They quickly attune to rhythmic tales told by an adult who also is enjoying its musical qualities. Some stories are structured primarily through word sounds and rhythms.

A flow of images: Other stories appeal more to our vision, presenting us with a stream of vivid pictures, sometimes with different layers of significance, like dreams. Giving yourself time to gaze at each section of the story, imagine a wonderful artist painting scenes and characters before your eyes. With practice the picture-language of the story will develop for you as if you are moving through an orderly gallery. Book illustrations often are dull by comparison with the pictures that can spring colorfully through active imagination. Our vision is linked to all our other senses.

A dance - form and direction: Stories move along in organized patterns. Recognizing these patterns helps us to remember their dance. A circular story moves steadily in one direction around

'The Mulberry Bush', always returning us safely to its original starting place. A spiral moves out and returns us along the same route, slightly or perhaps greatly changed. (*Pelle's New Coat* by Else Beskow is an outstanding picture book for becoming familiar with this pattern.) An accumulation story piles up to a finale containing all the details of the story, and sometimes reduces back again to the original form. *The Farmer in the Dell,* like many children's circle games, tells a story in a similar way to *The House that Jack Built, The Old Woman and Her Pig and The Gingerbread Man.* Linear stories move out toward a new destination, gaining strength sometimes through repetition, such as *The Three Billy Goats Gruff* and *The Three Little Pigs.* Most of the great fairy tales belong to this category. Unending tales are playfully open-ended, like 'Thousands of Ducks':

Once there was a farmer who owned thousands and thousands of ducks. One day he heard that there was to be a special holiday when lots of people would be in town and willing to buy. Since he had fallen on hard times the farmer decided to take his thousands and thousands of ducks to town to sell.

As he set out for town he came to a wide river. The bridge was far downstream – too far for the ducks to walk. The farmer saw a boat big enough to hold himself and two ducks. So he placed two of the ducks in the boat, climbed in and set off for the other shore. When he got these ducks safely to the other side, he rowed back to get two more ducks. He rowed them to the other side and went back for two more ducks. He rowed them to the other side and went back to get two more ducks.

(The storyteller can pause for the listener to ask 'What happened?' The teller replies 'He's still getting the ducks.')

Like a lid-box clicking shut, with the lesson of the story inside it, the *Jataka Tales* and the fables of Aesop and La Fontaine typically end with a moral. *The Folktale* by Stith Thompson identifies these and many other structures common to stories from around the world. Through the recognition of fundamental patterns, you can sense when your child requires one or another of them to assist their growth. Says one lively storyteller: ' The more I have learned stories the easier it is to learn them. The part of the memory that recognizes patterns develops the more I use it.'

Meaning and morals: Stories organized intentionally to explore realistic ideas and problems or to prove a point are mostly for older children. It is important to realize that very young children seldom remember stories merely rationally. They want to experience stories with their whole being. Infinitely more important to children than fiction stacked in their rooms is the quality of sharing they have with you.

Many storytelling parents are astonished when their children remember perfectly stories they have completely forgotten. Everyone can benefit from keeping a journal of the stories they share with their children. Noting a plot, or a particularly pleasing or puzzling bit can be useful in many ways to jog your memory now and in the coming years. Like your memory, your imagination is a living force. It can be an especially enlightening exercise to imagine your story characters coming to a castle or a cave in which there are pictures on the wall – each one alive. A character or perhaps a group of children step into the pictures. Afterwards they tell what was experienced on the other side. Very inspiring role models to enliven your imagination are – *The Wise Woman*, by George MacDonald, *The Chronicles of Narnia* by C.S. Lewis and *Mary Poppins* by P.L. Travers.

Creating Play

For young children actions often speak much more eloquently than words. Your storytelling brings them first of all into your presence. As they absorb the story, they are feeding upon qualities that stream through you. They commune with your sense of wonder and love. In all adults they seek ways of growing into a full and complete human being. Through listening well to stories, children:

• learn they can trust others to be present for them;
• go to a creative frontier with you - you model for them the creative process;
• experience the intensity, warmth and continuity of your adult attention;
• study the openness of your listening;
• learn your way with your words.

Your willingness to be playfully creative just for them nourishes and inspires them to be creative for and with others. How does adult creativity differ from a child's? The palette of faculties which adults draw from differs in quality and quantity from a child's. Our adult ego, developed over many years, is a relatively stable force. We have the ability to observe a creative process, to reflect upon it afterwards, to cherish it with consciousness. Little children jump and splash into the waters of life. Then the moment is over, and they jump into the next wave of creative participation.

As adults we must splash in with them to meet their needs and help them to face the future with observant and creative spirit. A woman with many academic achievements was extremely nervous about making up a story for her young daughter: she worried that it would not come out right and that she would fail miserably. Yet as she playfully practiced telling stories with other mothers, she began to relax and let go of her self-judgments. One day, her face flushed with wonder and excitement, she reported to the group that her daughter had received the story she told her the evening before as if she had been starved for it. This mother had arrived! It was the beginning of many realizations for her. She learned how and why to let her intuition be her guide in the stories she told, and within a year became a beloved teacher, known in her school as the only teacher who made up, rather than read stories.

Transforming well-known stories

Like shirts and shoes, stories told often can wear thin. It is an interesting experience to let a story go, perhaps for three weeks or for a year – and then to bring it back again intact and rested. To bring new energy to a very well-known story, a character or incident might be developed from an old story - a new shoot from the old stalk. A friend of mine included this anecdote in the fictional version of her childhood that she wrote when she was in her eighties:

One rainy day when a father and his son could not go fishing, the boy asked for a story and curled up beside his father on the sofa. 'Oh, not that old one,' he protested when the father began reading 'Little Red Riding hood' to him again.

'But this is one of the oldest stories in the world,' said his father, as he opened another book. 'Every country has it in some form. Here is a version I'm sure you never heard. It's about Red Riding hood's grandfather.'

'She had a grandfather?'

Then began a lively fresh spin off the old yarn. Father and son became happier as the story developed.

'The reason that you don't hear very much about the old man was that he was a tinker who traveled far and wide in the countryside, mending kettles and pans. He had a very small cart and a very small donkey to pull it. The cart was neatly fitted out with soldering iron, a small charcoal stove and all kinds of wire and nails. He had a small grindstone too and sharpened scissors and knives.' As the old man went on, he said the tinker dreamed one night that a great gray wolf stood by his bed, a beautiful creature with bright eyes.

The wolf spoke: 'We really are gentle animals. But a story of a wolf that ate an old woman has given us a bad reputation.' As the tinker stroked the wolf's head, the dream faded.
When the boy reached over to see if there were some more good stories in the book his father had been reading, he was surprised to see there was no writing at all. They were all blank pages.
'Dad, he cried, 'You made it all up.'
He twinkled. 'Well. It was a good story, wasn't it?'

As you make up original stories you might hold a book full of empty pages. Children also enjoy telling stories out of beautifully unwritten books. For inspiration you might read several versions of the same story, such as those found in Marian Cox's *Cinderella: Three Hundred and Forty-five Variants*.

Sounding the senses
Children seek the taste of truth, the aromas of human goodness and happiness. The grandfather of a friend of mine, a retired teacher, came to live with him and his family when he was six years old. Determined that his grandchildren would learn to enjoy their fundamental senses, as he had learned to do during his British childhood, this lively old gentleman always introduced his stories playfully, demonstrating the various senses with his special

routine. First he would pull his ear, then tweak his nose, wink one eye and then the other, stick out the tip of his tongue and, finally, balance himself precariously on one leg of his chair! This never failed to inspire the children's wonder and uproarious laughter. Then he would ask them with which of the senses they would like to play. If the children said 'Touch', they would play 'Blindman'. The children would tie a scarf around his eyes. Then his grandchildren would bring things to him in a basket. 'Don't bring me easy things like a cup or spoon.' He insisted that they hunt all over the house. Their mother helped them gather macaroni, a thimble, a needle-threader. Then the children and grandfather would reverse roles.

They also challenged one another with fascinating sounds by taking turns with closed eyes to identify the tinkle of a glass tapped by a pencil, the scraping of a carrot on a grater, the tick of a metronome. When they played 'Smells', the boy's mother provided spice boxes, crushed geranium leaves, lavender. The grandfather puzzled the children with the scents of old storybooks. 'Taste' was the favorite game, with nibbles of all sorts. Playing 'Sight', the old man would lay out a tray full of articles for the children to study, then cover them with a cloth.

As part of this game the grandfather would produce treasures from his old possessions, and tell his grandchildren a little about each one. Or he would make up a story, or transform a well-known one, to accentuate the particular sense they had chosen to enjoy. Our sense of smell can open up all our other senses. Include in a story some of the aromas your child experiences on a typical day indoors and out.

Story and song
A poem well loved by my aunt says:
Start to sing as you tackle the thing
That cannot be done – and you'll do it.

Music helps children make transitions. A mother, who was dismayed at her son's resistance whenever she wanted to go anywhere with him, let herself sing lilting songs from her own childhood and others she made up. The songs eased him into new activities where plain words could not. Eventually she also learned to sing him in and out of stories.

Like all the elements of stories that contribute to a sense of well-being, music increases the sense of rhythmic flow and balance. A group of parents encouraged one another to include singing in bedtime stories for their children. One working mother returned home to her children and sang her way through *The Frog Prince* as a little grand opera. 'I am with adults all day long, and I prefer to sing stories with my children. I discovered that singing doesn't drain me as talking does,' she said. The children, who already knew the story well, sometimes joined in with gleeful fascination. It brought energy and good humor to them all. After several days of practice, another mother reported: 'When I let myself hum a simple melody at the beginning of a story, it clears the air and helps my breathing. It makes me feel more present.' Said another, 'I live so much in my head.

Music covers my whole body like a blanket. It helps me find my heart and soul. Simple notes carry me along with the children to a sacred place. Afterwards we often remember the singing more than the plot.' Another reported to her storytelling circle: 'I realize now that my daughter and I are able to absorb tones much more easily than words. When I am singing simple words and melody I become more relaxed. If I am anxious about what is to happen next in the story, singing or humming for a moment invites the muse.'

A mother decided to join a singing group to take her over 'the hump of embarrassment' singing had caused her since childhood. A melody soon occurred to her as she was reading aloud to her children. She plucked up courage to sing a small rhymed section in the story. When the rhyme recurred, she repeated the simple three notes of its melody. The children snuggled closer and sang with her. She was excited to realize her music had helped the children join in and feel more part of the story. Several days later she ventured to make up another melody. Three or four gliding notes expressed 'swaying treetops'. It seemed so easy. She created a character who sang every morning on his walk as he walked into town to check the time on the village clock and on his return home by the same route. 'I would love a routine like that,' she sighed. 'If he is annoyed or distracted he returns to his song no matter what.' As time went on, she gained confidence, singing portions of stories before increasingly large audiences. 'I am always surprised even now how much children and adults respect and enjoy my singing,' she says, ' even though I sometimes do not sing in tune. It enchants us and carries our souls to a different reality. When I feel anxious about what will happen next my singing opens up the next inspiration.'

Speaking about creating music in the midst of life, a parent mused: 'I love to imagine the moon singing to a stone or to a rose.

Doesn't everything in nature sing, more than speak? I try to make the melody of a crow landing, or a deer running. When the children participate in the songs of starlight, clouds, stones, we become very happy together. Gentle singing helps us to sense their inaudible music.'

To enhance sung and spoken words, the ancient way of the storyteller often included instruments. The open strings of a lyre stir and expand our breathing before, during and after a story. For storytelling with small children, a friend made for me a tiny lyre with five strings that just fits in the palm of my hand. Many parents sound a small xylophone, or strike a bell or small cymbals at the beginning and the ending of a story. These resonate with firmer strokes, helping to shape a ceremonious sense of expectation and finality. Drums stimulate physical energy and can be disturbing to young children whose ears are awakening to the subtleties of spoken words, yet my clown doll likes to shake a tambourine to announce his stories. A wooden flute also pours out simple melodies and helps create bird-song and the sounds of wind and water. Children who know a story well enjoy adding the sounds of instruments they are given or that they make, such as polished stones and carved sticks struck together. Humming, singing or whistling a musical chorus to the storyteller's words summons joy.

Like all the elements of stories that contribute to a sense of well-being, music increases rhythmic flow and balance. Pure music can also stimulate the imaginations of children. A four-year-old friend of mine liked to place books full of famous paintings on the piano shelf and play songs about them: birds, sixteenth century Madonnas, and landscapes were her favorite images for musical reveries. A father encouraged his seven-year-old twins to make up stories as he played the piano. In this way they learned to be playfully sensitive to major and minor modes and to enjoy the interplay of tones and images. At seven years of age they were delightfully competent musicians and storytellers.

Each time words are repeated in a story, try singing those words simply and spontaneously. Gentle singing helps children and all of us to sense the inaudible music of stones, plants and animals, of clouds and starlight, of all living things. If you collect a basketful of simple musical instruments and teach your children to use them sensitively, they will enhance key moments in stories.

Tales with fingers and feet

Children eagerly imitate. When they learn to move their hands and fingers with a story, its content dances through to their fingertips and toes. Stories can spring out of your hands for them, as with the rabbit you see pictured here.

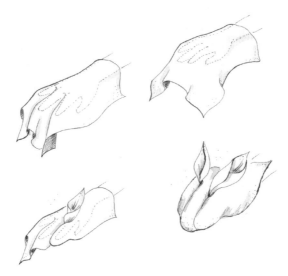

A fun-loving friend of mine tells stories to her four children with the help of Miss Tiddle-de-Dee, a toothless old woman with a comical high-pitched voice. She appears when the mother tucks her thumb inside her hand, which becomes Miss Tiddle-de-Dee's lower jaw. Then she ties a handkerchief over her hand, and sometimes adds two dots for eyes on the knuckle of her first finger. Silly and preachy, Miss Tiddly D. opens up her jaw-thumb wide to sing her raucous songs. 'I have so much fun with her.' said my friend. 'One day Miss T. got all dressed up in a white yarn wig and red lipstick, and caused wild laughter.' With a lively perspective on the children, she compliments them on their behavior and activities saying: 'Oh, that reminds me of a story', or 'When I was a girl about your age…' Their mother says: 'The children ask for her at bedtime or on train and road trips when they are restless. Her handy old helper bargains with them, saying, 'If you do as I say now and brush your teeth, I will tell you another story.'

A group of parents learned how to make felt. With the felt they formed and sewed small puppets to fit on their fingers and big toes. Many amusing story experiences with them ensued which their children joyously imitated.

Drawing and painting

Happy children radiate a full spectrum of fresh and subtle colors; fresh colors swirl around them. As storytellers, all our words are connected with the world of color. Yellow words dance lightly and brightly. Red words move us more vigorously, commanding and muscular. Green words flow smoothly in even regular tones. Blue and purple words rise from deep wells. Sparkling, crystal words send spirit light to a child. The palette of your speech can be richly varied. Like an artist applying colors to a canvas, you can place your words gently, vigorously, lightly, thoughtfully.

A story can be told in any of four fundamental energy patterns. Earth offers its deep thoughtfulness; air its bright, light playfulness; water its flowing, round fullness; or fire its vigorous muscular command. Beyond each one can be found a luminous balance that includes them all.

Your child has individuality and temperament and so do you. Several parents met to experiment with the creating of stories in different color moods. 'You can attract your child's attention and win their trust,' I offered, 'by matching the energy in your voice at the start of a story to her predominant mood. Then gradually move the story in the direction of harmony and balance.' As the group thought of their children in terms of energy and color, stories began to come to them. One mother painted red, red and more red with her temperamental six-year-old daughter. Then she told a story which began: 'Once there was a princess named Ruby. Her hair was red as fire. She was a princess of great beauty and also of great temper.' Painting and story together calmed them both down. At the end they painted a beautiful shade of soothing green that balanced the red. The green moved her to end the story with balanced words that surprised and deeply pleased them both:

The peasant and the princess sprinkled themselves with the evergreen water of the stream, and bravely, hand in hand, they walked through the blazing hot flames. And when they had reached the other side of the fire, before them grew a magnificent red rose.

Pick the Rose
For soon you shall be wed,
The nurturing green
To the passion of red

The king greeted the couple with great joy, and blessed their union, and they lived together in great harmony and happiness.

Another mother painted nothing but yellows one afternoon with her children. She wanted to create a dance of words and imagery that would reflect their paintings. After a while she began a story.

Once upon a time there was land of Yellow, a place of bright rolling hills and meadows. The women there were light-hearted and smiling, cooking and cleaning and singing as they worked. The men were nimble farmers, painters, drivers of milk trucks, hardly stopping except to eat a small meal and give short thanks for it. Children flitted about hiding and seeking, excitedly climbing to the upper and outer-most branches of shining trees.

With so much yellow in her mind, she began to long for a balancing color and gave the children glowing purple paint and crayons. After a time she finished her story:

When the land took time finally to rest, the purple protective glow of the moon covered it with quiet calm, giving the land strength to start its next busy day.

Drawing and painting, we become sensitive to shapes and hues. With a little adult guidance children learn to recognize in the colors many different moods. A sad, a shy, or a crowded tree can tell its story. Trees, mountains and flowers can dance together in the sunrise to celebrate a new day. A pensive rainbow can brood beneath a cloud when a beloved parent or friend is away. Especially for the youngest children, crayons can become little emanations of the realities they represent. You can create with your child a big Golden Father Sun crayon waking up and leaving behind a glowing picture on the page. A little bird crayon flies through the air onto the page; a worm crayon wriggles out for a walk. The up and down movement of a brush or crayon can become a tree climbing slowly to the sky, an eager bean plant or a drooping daffodil. The pace, direction and pressure of your crayon or brush each tell a silent story. The colors you choose can hide, sleep, stretch, climb, burst, smile, dance.

Picture-making can also create a feeling for the fundamental structure of a story as a whole. Three pages, one each for its beginning, development, and ending, sewn together into a little 'book', provide a foundation for retelling the whole story. I have found that when I draw or paint a simple, clear image from a story as I am telling it, children develop an eye for form. Their imaginations come alive as they try for their own colorful expression of the gestures of animals, plants and human characters. I like to use the broad sides of crayons and wide brushes. These help children avoid the stress of finding exact outlines and proportions of things, requiring skills beyond their needs and ability. Broad-brushed images also help them feel the form they are making as a whole.

Fill yourself with a sense of yellow or red or blue or green light, until you can feel it in your breath and permeating the air around you. Now begin a story about a character in that color mood. Let your words stay true to its light, as it weaves through your thoughts and feelings. Observe how your child adapts to different color moods.

Board games
Young children can, with your help, also turn stories into games. Making game boards deepens children's awareness of story patterning. As they paint or draw a game-board and make little characters to move along its pathways, details of the story will flow through them again and again. Dice from wax or wood, and number spinners, are easy to make.

Favorite stories such as *The Three Bears* or *The Three Little Pigs* can be visualized for young children as cooperative board games. These are a delight for both adults and children to play together. A family with children ranging in age from three to nine years old enjoyed games and worked together with their mother to make a board game at Christmas to share with their friends. They loved the story of *Old Befana* and painted the main events of the story on a large sheet of paper glued onto cardboard, The path of her journey was made with potato prints in the shape of stars.

Another family created a large game-board of *Hansel and Gretel* and the path the children took through the dark wood. They made a three-dimensional witch's oven painted from cardboard, with a fluffy orange flame in it of painted sheep's wool. Hansel and Gretel, the mother and father, the witch and the white bird were made of beeswax, stabilized underneath by flat buttons. The rules were simple in this cooperative game. With each roll of the dice, the players could move any character along the path until the children were returned on the duck's back to their beloved father on the far side of the water, and the story was complete.

Dancing a story

Impressionable children tend to imitate the movements that surround them. A spiraling leaf, a flapping crow, a leaping grasshopper, a racing dog – any movement in the natural world that draws your child's attention can provide a vivid starting point for a story.

A white cat came every morning to drink at a pond. One summer morning a mother decided to transform this lovely familiar scene into an imagination: 'Once upon a time a white cat drank from the Waters of Life.' Three seven year old girls who were best friends play-acted a long story in movement about the cat, which they imagined to be an enchanted princess. Their story play lasted for hours. They found flowing cloths, large rhubarb leaves and other props to enhance their movements. At the end of the afternoon the children invited their parents to see their story in action, taking turns narrating as the others danced it out.

A friend of mine plays 'Grandfather Plants a Turnip Seed' with her children and their friends. Each time a child who is chosen to be the seed sits, while another chosen to be Grandfather pats the earth around the seed. Then they sing:

> *Grandfather plants a turnip seed, hi diddle dee*
> *He plants it in the earth so deep, high diddle dee.*

[Grandfather gestures with his arms to show how big the turnip

grows as they sing:]
   Grow my turnip big and sweet
   Grow my turnip grow.
[The grandfather places his hands on the turnip's shoulders and tries to pull.]
   Grandfather goes to pull it out, hi diddle dee
   But turnip is so big and stout, hi diddle dee.
   Grandmother quickly come to me, you help me pull.
   Ha rook ha rook ha rook dee rook —
   The Turnip will not move.
[The grandmother places her hands on the grandfather's shoulders and tries to pull. They rock gently back and forth, then gesture to a child.]
   The grandmother calls to the grandchild, you help me pull.
   He rook he rook he rook dee rook
   The turnip will not move
   The grandchild calls to the dog. The dog calls to the cat.
   *The cat calls to the mouse, you help me pull_*
   The mouse comes running one two three
   And pulling strong as he can be
   He rook ha rook ha rook plop! Now the turnip's out!
[The mouse joins the line, and they all fall down together.]

   Tra la la la la la la la la tra la la la —
   Tra la la la la la la la la tra la la
They sing as the game ends in a circle to gain a sense of order once more. Sometimes there are many children in the neighborhood outdoors together. Then the mother helps more than one turnip and grandfather start their own lines.

Another mother who loves dancing discovered a multitude of movements to go along with her children's favorite stories. They would mime *The Shoemaker and the Elves*, sewing with long threads, and loudly or softly counting his stitches. She and her children loved the swift-footed, lively little elves; she imagined them before and after their visit to the old shoemaker's house, dancing as they prepared to do golden deeds – and afterward. Mother and children together created little elfin dances, which they repeated many times. Turning *The Little Red Hen* into a dancing story in the living-room of their house, they soon knew it, even the youngest, down to their toes. Both she and her children were happiest when a story flowed into movement. A family friend, who was a playful violinist, sometimes provided background music for the stories. At Halloween, she created creaky notes, as little witches who did not brush their teeth dressed in outlandish garbs, zigzagged on their broomsticks, stirred their pots, slurped worms, and popped frogs and spiders into their bags.

Playacting

Retelling a story can become a grand occasion. A family of children asked their mother to stay out of the room, until they rang a bell. When she was finally allowed to enter, she found them all dressed for the story and seated at attention. She realized with what ceremony they wanted to listen to the marvelous story she would tell.

After a little encouragement children readily turn stories into plays. Play-acting begins to prepare children for the many dramas ahead in the very real stories of their inner and outer lives. As they embody different characters and scenes of the story, they grow into it, and make it their own. A young father decided to arrange his schedule so he could be at home three mornings a week with his children. Over many months he was astonished at the inspiration stories provided. He happily admitted: 'It is really very good for me too, letting the images stream through us as a family!'

Children quickly learn they can become any character or part of a story, with simple colorful costumes, a basket of hats, capes that can be easily put on and off. After she had read them a story, a home-schooling mother's young children acted out stories every morning at home. She generously reserved a corner of the living room closet for intriguing items: shoes, masks, poles, collapsible boxes to be made into huts and palaces. The children would eagerly decide who would become each character, and as their mother retold the story they would take parts or assign them to household things: a broom the golden bird, this ladder a tree, that cloth-covered lamp a mountain. Sometimes when other members of their extended family were present, she would say: 'Go make up a play for us, children' and give them a hat or two and a box filled with interesting items to include in the story they would make up to enact for the adults who were present.

Parents who enter fully into play can experience the joy of sharing a child's world again. Young children usually want their elders to take the parts that frighten them. A group of families made a story parade with puppet costumes and masks to represent different aspects of the Grimms' tale *The Wolf and the Seven Little Kids*. To celebrate Halloween they moved through their neighborhood singing merrily. Some of the adults were costumed as wolves and all the children wore goats' masks they had created together. The parents carried bright torches as the 'little kids' cavorted and danced. The story gave the whole evening a festive coherence. Many neighbors came outdoors, entranced to see this unusually orderly, happy and powerful spectacle. The parade ended with a potluck feast to which each family contributed.

Two American families with children ranging from five to twelve years old decided to visit El Salvador. These families had attended the outdoor summer productions of a gigantic puppet theater for

several years, taking in many impressions from its artistic and powerful productions. The children, who wanted to bring something enjoyable to the families they would meet on their journey, decided to create their own puppet production of *The Three Billy Goats Gruff* – a story with subtle political overtones. They practiced the story in Spanish. Before their departure they made simple, easy-to-carry puppets on sticks for the goats and the troll, and painted a back-cloth of the story landscape to drape over a clothesline, a portable theater that would be easy to suspend in the villages they were to visit. The children used battery lamps to spotlight the events of the story. Each time the goats went over the bridge, the village children would join with international glee in their 'trip trop trip trop' song.

Together with cousins or neighbors, you too might create a play out of a story. Send hand-lettered invitations. Bake delicious refreshments that relate to the story such as cakes in the shape of crowns. Make simple puppets to represent characters in a story, perhaps moving them through an imaginary landscape of colored cloths. The play will help children build up and organize imagination to feed all of their faculties.

Embroider and sew

A mother who loved sewing while her young children played, wanted to make wall-hangings for both her young daughters as birthday gifts. She decided to portray the main characters of their favorite stories with colored pieces of felt, silk and cotton. As the children watched her sew these gifts for them, she retold the stories many times. They soon knew by heart the stories she was portraying with her patient needlework. As teenagers they insist on keeping these murals in their rooms.

A multitude of dolls, puppets and costumes can give dimension and texture to your child's imagination. *The Mary Francis Sewing Book* by Jane Fryer presents sewing lessons as a long story. Thimble People and a Sewing Bird introduce a young girl, through a combination of riddles, verses and imaginative conversations, to the pleasures of sewing many different kinds of stitches. They show her how to follow patterns to create various delightful garments and hats. Its many characters include a laughing pincushion and dancing pins, needles and buttons.

Story aprons

A story apron can provide children with their first theater experience. Peek-a-boo pockets, hide treasures that can appear and then disappear again as if behind a curtain. A simple story apron, symbolic of all that is hidden within your children, can help you to celebrate a season, a birthday or other special occasion.

A mother who enjoys theater arts and sewing has created several such aprons for herself and her daughters over the years. When her children were three- and four years old, she shaped pockets to match the stories that hid inside them: an egg-shaped pocket held a little chicken, a tree-green pocket an elf, a milk-white pocket a little cow. At the approach of spring one year, she filled an apron

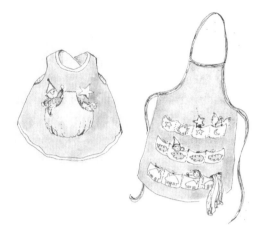

with bells, birds, and finger-puppet flowers, each with its own little story and song. In autumn another mother made an apron with many little pockets to contain seeds, butterfly and other little signs of autumn that emerged as she told their stories. An apron with felt earthworms and insects in its pockets helped her to sing playfully and tell her little sons their stories.

Using a sturdy weight of deep blue cotton, a mother designed and sewed an apron with pockets large enough to hold many different colored scarves. The colors helped her family to build up story landscapes – a red scarf became the rising sun, a blue scarf, a flowing ocean, a rose-colored scarf a cloud dancing with the wind. As their stories ended, the colors flowed back into their original pockets. Inspired by the freedom of imagination she experienced with her children and their friends, she decided to sew a midnight blue apron with twelve pockets. During 'the twelve days of Christmas', a gift emerged from each of the pockets – a shepherd's lamb, a starry stone, a harmonica, juggling balls – each with its own story for the holy nights.

A story bag or basket provides a similar method for bringing a variety of stories out at the request of a child. A number of pockets can be sewn around the edge of a big basket in which story objects can rest until story time, perhaps pictures of family members who live far away, or representations of other important people and places to surface from time to time. The pockets in a father's work-apron were transformed to hold magic tricks. His children have learned which trick lives in which one: they point and ask for them. Their Magic Master's tricks, like puppets, have a life of their own. He will listen and look carefully as they emerge: 'This trick wants you first to answer the riddle in my story' he might say or 'This puzzle wants me first to tell you children a very puzzling story.'

Whether you wear a pocket-filled apron, or keep your stories under a cloth inside a basket or in a pouch, you will be supporting children as they develop and organize their imaginations. It is often wise to keep adult story-making items separate to help children freely imitate adult creativity in their own way.

Questions you may be asking
1. Do you believe you are not a storyteller?
   As a parent or grandparent, you have an innate right to be a storyteller. Don't give up! As you practice, the stories and the children will give you more and more confidence.

2. Do you become fascinated by the story and lose touch with your child?
   Remember that the story belongs to everyone.

3. Do you fear your stories will not be as good as book stories?
   Who would not choose to introduce children to the best? Yet children sense sincere creative effort. They love this as a reflection of their own growing and striving, as this smacks of life! Like learning to play an instrument, storytelling can be a

gradual process. Fearful perfectionism is worth overcoming again and again.

4. Do you sense that you are telling too many stories?
Make story times regular daily, weekly, seasonal events. Sing, hum, knit, bake, saw, build, repair, surround the child with nonverbal rhythmic activities to satisfy their daily need for closeness with you.

5. Does your child want more books?
Retell book stories to children, sometimes in your own words. Make books with and for them out of stories they already know. As you hand-letter and illustrate these books, you help them understand the astonishing process of book production. Slowing down to create books, children build crucial hand and eye coordination. Activating their creativity supports them body and soul to assimilate the substance of any good story.

6. Does your young child want to read and write more than listen to stories?
Children naturally want to imitate adults. Increase contact with people who work well with their hands and bodies: grocers, builders, dancers, musicians, gardeners, orchard keepers, animal lovers. Write intimate and child-centered cards, letters and storybooks about these people .

7. Do you doubt your voice is adequate to your child's needs?
Make your voice an instrument of love, truth, courage, joy. Attend to every word you say, especially during a story, and enjoy the deep commitment and the spirit of adventure this inspires. Through stories we discover the faithful creative powers in which we live and speak, and the vastness of our hearts.

4 Stories for Growth and Change

Look well, therefore, to this day.
Sanskrit Hymn

Wisdom springs from life experience, well-digested.
Eric Erikson

Stories for Unborn Children

Evidence from many sources suggests that even before they have been born, children are influenced by their parents' activities, attitudes and thoughts. Is it ever too early to cradle children with wise stories? Reliable adult wisdom can hold even the unborn with warmth and love. What can be said to children about a caterpillar, germinating seeds, or an egg?

As adults most of us feel bound into diminished stories of who we are, have been and can be. Yet the time before a new child is born is an opportunity to practice speaking of the human family and of our own immediate families with respect and hope. When we speak with clarity and warm caring generosity, the minds and hearts of children tend to flourish; and those same attitudes tend to emerge from them.

To summon a loving and creative spirit, Louis MacNeice listened for the voice of his coming child and wrote "Prayer Before Birth":

> *I am not yet born; provide me*
> *With water to dandle me, grass to grow for me, trees to talk*
> *   To me, sky to sing to me, birds and white light*
> *   In the back of my mind to guide me . . .*
> *I am not yet born; O fill me*
> *With strength against those who would freeze my*
> *Humanity . . .*

Mothers and fathers often invite Brother Blue, 'the grandfather of storytelling' in America, to tell story-songs to the spirits of their coming children: 'I see you in your mama, little sailor. God is telling your story.' With the joyous and luminous power of jazz he sings about the world that is waiting to greet and play with them, and the love that holds them: 'You can play peek-a-boo with everything that is – the stars, the trees, the seas.' He croons a litany of creatures, plants and earth, all humbly awaiting the child.

Sensing that much is being learned in embryo, many parents speak to their coming children, or read, silently and aloud, perhaps in more than one language about what they hope will be important to them. A cellist practiced a beloved concerto every day while carrying her son. When he grew up to become a conductor, he discovered that he had an intimate knowledge of the concerto music she had been memorizing during his gestation, without ever having studied it himself.

I recently joined a circle of adults of all ages who wanted to shower a first-time mother and the coming child with gifts and stories. Each of us had been invited to think about our relationship with her. A variety of wild and cultivated flowers and carefully chosen objects were placed in the center of the circle. At the young mother's side was an old family cradle. As we took turns telling memories of times we had shared with her that highlighted her mothering qualities – patience, humor, generosity, wit – our stories stirred tears, laughter and joyous tenderness. A scribe, chosen among us for skill in calligraphy, lettered each quality spoken of onto a broad ribbon. As our anecdotes ended, mother, grandmothers, aunts and other guests placed tangible gifts into the cradle to represent the stories we had told, together with the flowing ribbon of golden words. You too might create a celebration for a newborn, or for the baby you once were.

The Earliest Years

Each new birth represents both very personal experience and a grand expanse of human history. Alexander Eliot in his book *The Universal Myths* describes a custom of the Osage Indians. When a new child is born to them, they summon a man who 'has talked with the gods' to recite the creation of the universe. When the baby wants to drink water and is old enough to eat solid food, the same storyteller is called each time to recite their myth of creation of water; or of the origin of grains. Although such rituals and cosmic storytellers are rare today, nevertheless much can be done to create them out of ourselves.

Journals for newborns

Although she was lacking the support of an inspired and disciplined communal storyteller, a young mother resolved to make a book about the gestation and early years of each of her children. From the outset she kept her journals to give to her children when they were preparing to give birth to their own babies. 'You are there,' the first of her journals tenderly began. She recorded the art and the thoughts she was attracted to during the pregnancy, her prayers and meditations and the books she was reading, her birthing classes and her daughter's arrival. Later this precious document evoked many heartfelt conversations between them. For her second child, a son, she also wrote the first words of her journal in golden letters: 'This book is to record the mystical joy of participating in your creation. I want you to know someday about the moments as they come and go. I want to be known as your agent of creation. May you always be free to be an individual.' As the babies grew to be toddlers, she added descriptions of amusing and trying incidents with them. They were sometimes written hastily in tired but loving moments, yet each one became an important treasure for them in later years.

Another mother adopted a nine-month-old child, Molly. As soon as she arrived, the mother decided to write the story of the child's life to present it to her later. After a few months had passed, she sewed a doll to resemble her daughter. The child learned to iron and sew for this little companion; they dressed in a similar way and explored the outdoors together. After their walks, mother and child would draw in a book what they had seen, singing and speaking about horses, clouds, flowers and trees in all seasons. The mother wrote about their favorite sights and sounds in the book. When visitors arrived, the girl would say: 'Would you like to hear the Molly Book?' Then she would turn the pages for them and retell her adventures with her mother and her beloved doll.

To young children, stories are living experiences. It is easy to forget how abstract a book is, so removed from the things and activities it represents. As adults conditioned to mechanically printed words on dry rectangular pages, we can easily forget how young children experience words as alive. Anything can become their plaything and turn into a story, whether captured in writing or not. Before their vision shrinks to printed pages, they enjoy telling or listening to a story based on anything they see, or 'reading' a random series set out before them – acorns, stones, feathers…

It can be a delightfully rewarding experience to bind together your own and your child's pictures as 'storybooks' without written words, using needle and thread and colorful ribbons. An artistic friend of mine realized that her daughter did not at all need written words to enjoy a story. She began to paint very simple watercolor pictures of her daughter's favorite places and animal friends. Later she glued several of these paintings together and folded them accordion-style. The book, with its accumulation of shining colorful images on sturdy paper, stood almost as large and tall as her child was. As she opened and arranged it in a circle on the floor, it completely surrounded the little girl. The mother moved around outside the book to speak beautifully about each picture. Soon her daughter was doing the same, sometimes turning in the midst of the circle of pictures as she spoke, sometimes moving beautifully around it from outside, like her mother.

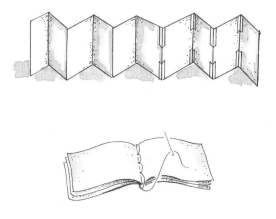

Together and Alone: All Are One

Respectfully surrendering with our children to the truth of nature invites an endless flow of images. With them we grow increasingly familiar with the stones, plants, animals, and human activities in their immediate surroundings – rainbow bursting from crystal; budding hawthorn; golden kittens' eyes. As their imaginations awaken, our senses naturally join them to range forth on journeys of discovery.

A beloved American classic, *Opal: The Journal of Opal Whiteley* portrays the desire of children to name and befriend everything. An orphan child of genius, Opal gave her animal friends names she found in a book that had been left to her by her beloved parents. Her favorite mouse she called Felix Mendelssohn, her dearest pig Peter Paul Rubens; William Shakespeare was her horse. Of a lonely walk in a field she wrote in her unique seven-year-old poetic style:

I have thinks these potatoes here do have knowings of star songs. I have kept watch in the field at night and I have seen the stars look kindness down upon them. And I have walked between the rows of potatoes and I have watched the star gleams on their leaves…

When I feel sad inside, I talk things over with my tree. I call him Michael Raphael. It is a long jump from the barn roof into his arms. It is such a comfort to nestle up to Michael Raphael. He is a grand tree. He has an understanding soul.

From birth, children relate naturally to others who love and take care of one another. The Sun, Earth, Stars and Moon can be spoken of as a loving family enfolding them. With growing sensitivity to their natural surroundings, even very small children today increasingly experience themselves as universal beings who are in touch with our whole earth, its global family and surrounding planetary and stellar worlds. They will speak of this to us adults if we are willing to listen without interposing our own ideas. I vividly remember finding a place to dig through to the other side of the world with my brothers, when we were very young. I can still feel our joy, when we thought we had seen the hair of a new playmate appearing in the earth under our feet, like a strange and friendly flower.

The archetypal language of stories naturally broadens our perspectives. As you read or tell a story to your own children, imagine that you are simultaneously sharing it with children throughout the world. A Chinese-American storyteller says that the western stories her mother shared, as if seeding a garden, helped her to grow and adapt to the different cultures she encountered during her difficult, unsettled childhood. She proves, through her sensitive multi-cultural spirit, that broad and varied listening, even at a very young age, can bear good fruit in later years. Many parents believe that children should hear stories from all around the world at an early age. Yet learning to appreciate such stories will of course be a lifetime process. Young children can bask in words and music without understanding them. Over months and years their ears learn to distinguish syntax and meaning, language and culture. No one can predict how a child will absorb and recreate the music of stories rich in sound and folk wisdom.

Stories Nurture Healthy Development

Vulnerable moments, moments of growth

At certain times throughout childhood there comes a complex drive towards independence, and a loosening of secure patterns. As children push adults away, they often experience our rejection - just when reassuring closeness is needed. Much of our insecurity and weakness as adults can stem from such moments. I once visited a friend whose son was turning seven years old. As I entered the room, I felt a strong sense of protection and birth. She had been holding him for hours, enfolded in a warm blanket, telling him stories. He had tried to curl into her lap with his big growing body, and she had responded with unusual sensitivity and patience. Although he was not ill, she did not embarrass him for wanting to feel himself wrapped in an old blanket for a long time within her embrace, protected like an embryo or newborn baby. The stories he first asked his mother to tell him were about his birth. Then he wanted to hear about all his earlier years, the worst and the best he had done, and to recall some of the stories he used to love, coming not from books, but directly from her. The boy is now a teenager with inner sturdiness. He is a natural leader at school. Kind and insightful, he is able to remember patiently what others have forgotten about people and events, and to find warm perspectives for the future.

Not all children have the good fortune to be embraced by their own 'story mother' and helped at crucial turning points to review their lives. Yet, along with their elders, children are compelled to go back over their lives periodically, to prepare for new growth. As they alternately draw near to mother and father and then push away, children need warmth, patient insight and caring words. Although they may seem to close down into a deep protective slumber, children become especially open and sensitive during periods of growth,. As they experience times of contraction, and hiding and dreaming of unknown times, they need more sleep, shelter, privacy and simplicity. Like every one of us, they can experience deep sadness as old ways inevitably pass. When I was twenty-one years old, I felt myself to be changing in complex, compelling ways, and wanted to live quietly in black dresses; I knitted a black shawl. I was like a chrysalis in a dark cocoon, clinging to a deeply stirring sense of the future. Consoling and enlivening pictures for such deep processes live in the natural world. We can emerge from a period of contraction and privacy as if a skin has been shed or an eggshell broken open.

Growth is a continuous adventure story. Stories that portray the truth of natural rhythms can help move us on. During children's many large and small spirals of growth, we can observe beautiful complex growth rhythms, supporting them through our imagination. Both creative forces, that build and sustain, and destructive forces, that break down the old, help them to find evolutionary pathways. Your own original stories drawn from nature, together with a flow of traditional imaginative stories that embody creation and transformation, can support, challenge and help them accept every stage of their development. An adult with openness and deep interest in fairy tale lore can create a listening heart, which will traverse out worn territories and leave picture-language still powerful and intact. New stories containing both old and new elements can arise naturally from these old imaginations.

Sometimes little children who are not yet ready for fairy tales picture changes vividly in their dreams, which during spurts of growth tend to be lively and disturbing. Visions and traces of memory from many sources can make an appearance. When children are disturbed by their dreams, a simple positive story about a dreamer can reassure them:

Once there was a new little tree that was dreaming of being a big tree. After a long time of growing, it became that very tree. And when it was big it could see very far over the valley and many birds sang happily in its branches.'

Or *'Once upon a time, a little stone dreamed it could dance and a child picked it up and skipped it far out across the great lake; then the waves danced it back to the shore.*

Butterflies and seeds portray growing patterns, which can gently and vividly reflect the children to themselves. The lively little sleeping seeds inside an apple are in touch with the whole tree, dreaming its eternal nature and how to release themselves again. 'I have a long way to go today,' a seed might shout in a story you tell, as it is flung from its pod. Or a graceful little maple seedling might seek companions to chat with, in seed-speech, about life's challenges. A vulnerable seedling finds a formidable obstacle course as it grows: rocks, stones, old lilac roots, acidic streams, tired earth. Some push through for a lonely time before they reach the light and can be greeted and celebrated by what lives in the upper world: soft winds, singing birds...

Small children can increasingly discover plants and animals as their companions in the adventure of growing. A group of parents whose children were about to go to school planted imaginative seeds. *Once there was a little tree. One night, when the moon was very bright, it grew down and it grew up, and in the morning light, all its branches and twigs felt very different,* began one mother's tale. Another began:

A little cloud drifted merrily, following the bigger clouds through the fields of sky. Then Father Sun said to the Little Cloud, 'It is time for you to grow.' But the Little Cloud didn't want to grow. It wanted to stay small and play in the sky. But nevertheless it began to grow. It cried out, 'Please, I want to be little.' But it continued to grow and puff until at last the Sun called, 'My Cloud child, you are truly magnificent. Now you can send showers to the gardens. Together we can hold a rainbow and the Earth happy.' And then the little cloud burst with joy.

The view from the crest of a wave of growth may sometimes reveal vistas of the future, a vivid glimpse of challenges ahead. Yet simultaneously there can be resistance. The greater the wave the more likely its forward surge will bring about a compelling backwash into familiar safety zones. A mother and four-year-old who lived by the sea were relieved after she put his reluctance to grow into a story that began:

Once there was a little ripple that stayed inside its big mother and father waves. But then it felt it was being filled up from the inside and it didn't want to grow bigger. It wanted to be a little ripple and flow along with them.

As children gather strength, they need to receive again and again a sense of security and connection. All children hunger for meaningful, friendly relations with the natural world. The respectful attention of our words toward the lives of creatures and their offspring helps a child turn embarrassment, over-excitement or repugnance inculcated by adult attitudes into serene, respectful acceptance. A simple factual story of a mother pig that must nurse twelve little piglets brings forth the beauty hidden in what might seem alarming. Neglect and suffering amongst animals, described with loving compassion, also helps children to build soul forces. They can be strengthened by descriptions of the simple steadiness of mates in nature, especially if their parents live separately. A story of ducks that are loyal to one another tells the child there is a form in the humble lives of little creatures toward which they can aspire.

Look for stories with images which your children can feel as reflections of their own growing. Try to create a story which contains hidden places where what was large becomes tiny or what was small becomes, even quite suddenly, large. You might try beginning a story with: 'Inside a tree lived a squirrel family', or ' Once there lived a little rabbit that wanted to be smaller and hide,' or 'Once upon a time there was a big caterpillar that wrapped itself up slowly and fell into a deep slumber.'

Opposition

New growth can be painful; as children mature, their first bouts of independence and self-consciousness can be daunting for everyone around them. Yet opposition to parental authority, a sign of the growing individuality, can be completely welcomed into stories. Opposition is the foundation for morality. Character and consciousness grow in the space between yes and no. Many of the wisest old fairy tales play between these poles. Stories allow us to contain the contradictory needs of a child, maintaining rules while at the same time acknowledging struggles and feelings. Stories flex, resist and rest. They engage musculature of soul that interpenetrates physical muscles. Children need muscular imagination. The paradox of resistance in the growth process tests the ingenuity of the child, who wants to be a good and acceptable family member. It also tests those who usually prefer to encourage and approve of their children, rather than restrain and reprimand them.

After many evening meals spent battling his youngest son into eating, a father had an inspiration. Although he was a taskmaster, he was also a witty storyteller. He discovered how to express his son's contradictory energies and bring them to a satisfying resolution. *Once there was a dinner that did not want to be eaten,* his story began. Paradox is typical of the wise old story realm.

The peas rolled out the door, the baked potatoes hid in their skins, and the fish leapt from the plate, turned into a bird and flew into the attic. The whole family cried. Now they had nothing to eat and their plates were empty. The next evening it happened as it had the previous day. At last the family was so hungry the father called 'Come back!' The mother called 'Come back!' and the child whispered, 'Please come back.' and the peas rolled onto the plates, the baked potatoes opened, the fish leapt onto the plate, and everyone sat and ate a nice dinner together.

As the story repeated, sometimes the names of the food changed. Using a story creatively to accept and enjoy the child's opposition to eating his dinner, peace arose for both the little boy and his father.

Push your arm or leg against a wall and let it go, and your arm or leg will rise blissfully by itself. Imaginative pictures, like a good wall, relieve children for a time of their need to push against adults in order to loosen their bodies and souls from former holding patterns, to let go and grow. Opposition and resistance in stories can cause deep and sometimes uproarious enjoyment for four- and five- year-old children. A family of three young children became very attached to *Sweet Porridge,* an ingenious and wise tale in the Grimms' collection about the development of self-control. In the story a little cooking pot produces more and more porridge until it fills a whole village. The mother helped her children to act out this story. Over and over again she became the pot, they the porridge bubbling noisily and wriggling around the room. At last one of the children would call out the magical words to make the magic pot stop cooking. As a result of repeatedly playing through this story, the children made joyous and significant strides in self-discipline.

The power of 'no'

The passionate 'no's of children's earliest years gradually transform into the ability to make choices and to launch freely into their own imagination. Simple tales of the 'no's' that pervade the earliest years can gradually turn into increasingly subtle imaginative stories. *Once a prince received a wise and magical horse,* a story might begin for a five-year-old child who does not like to do as he is told. Or *Once there was a gentle princess who knocked on every door of an old castle but no one opened* might begin a story for a six-year-old who is feeling neglected and lonely.

Although we may feel we would like to protect them forever from conflict, we also know children will oppose us in regular bouts in order to find independence and self-reliance. Each child must take on this maturational struggle. They partly create themselves out of antipathy toward the ways of parents and other adults. Their lively, although often unspoken, repugnance, driven by the momentum of evolution working through them, causes a creative search for alternatives. Discomfort with our adult mannerisms, attitudes and conversational style creates a longing for a reality closer to their heart's desire.

Like stories, children frequently embody the battleground of life into which they have been born. The majority of great tales contain opposing needs, attitudes and outlooks. Their resolution creates a sense of satisfaction at the end of the story. The elder sisters in *The Three Little Men in the Wood* say 'no' when the dwarfs ask for their help. The youngest, however, says 'yes' and out of this a kinder humanity dawns. Generous Simpleton surpasses his selfish brothers or sisters in the end and becomes a wise ruler. Opposing characters in stories help children to experience their own inner conflicts. They help them meet struggles with clear open hearts in their families, at school and with their friends. Behind many fairy tales lives great wisdom: conflict ends with increase of love and power to the protagonists who willingly and courteously do what must be done. This fundamental plot gives a blueprint on very deep levels for the awakening soul life of every child.

Careful and caring imaginative stories can help children bring healthy understanding to their own budding sexuality and power of choice. Well-spoken stories can help them absorb a beautiful clear 'no' to help them confront a variety of challenges. Their power of self-protection is hidden in this word, which will sound naturally from them when the wisdom in stories has helped develop it in them. As they absorb the power of the 'no' through imaginative pictures, they are helped to see their way through all kinds of situations, and to be less burdened by fear or terror.

A mother of two boys, aged four and six, lived in a city neighborhood from which a young boy had been perilously lured away. Many parents were worried and even hysterical. She decided to create a story to put this event into perspective for herself and the children. She intentionally chose to make the central character feminine to ease their imaginations.

Once upon at time there was a little princess and everyone loved her dearly. She found great joy in helping whoever she could. She lived a happy life and her parents loved her more than life. She was safe and happy at home in the castle, sometimes she would wander on her horse over the hillsides and through the valleys, speaking a friendly word to everyone she met. The people knew her and watched out for her. If there was a dangerous animal they would warn her and show her which way to go. If there was a thunderstorm, they would take her in and shelter her. If she had gone too far from home to return for dinner, they would feed her. Her parents knew that she was safe and word would always reach them of her whereabouts.

When the trusting child in her story suddenly encountered a threatening intruder,

the princess saw a little white angel on a tree branch shaking her head. With one movement, the girl coaxed her horse's head around, kicked him in the sides, and off they went as fast as the wind. Without looking back, they rode through the night and didn't stop until they reached her parents' castle. When she told them what had happened people were sent out all over the land to identify the intruder, who was nowhere to be found. The princess stopped spending so much time away from home and trusting everyone.

Many years later, a jester visited the castle and spoke about someone who lured children away, until a child would be strong and smart enough to realize the danger in time and say 'No' and run home. Then the intruder would lose his power. 'Maybe someone did,' the jester added. 'Because I haven't heard of stolen children here for a long time.'

This story helped the children and their parents to calm down. The mother lovingly guarded the silence at the end of the tale to allow the children's feelings and thoughts to unfold freely. The next day, as the deep power of the story took effect, she simply told the story to the children again. On other days neighborhood children listened too. How different this was from repeating in a flat and fearful voice to her boys, 'Never go with strangers.' The story included both trust and caution, and gave balance to the power of *yes* and *no*.

When a story is kept on the imaginative level, you can include elements of opposition which offer resolutions to a conflict in your child's life. The story patterning of such stories as *Sweet Porridge* empower children to grow through their command of words.

Stories and Moral Development

Can stories inspire us to become wise? How do imaginative stories support the desire to be good and to establish positive relations with the surrounding world? An increasing number of storytelling parents and educators are actively asking these questions.

Writers of children's stories with powerful moral fiber can stimulate our own storymaking and storytelling. I ponder the stories created by the Scottish visionary, George MacDonald, who raised thirteen children. I study old and more modern fairy tales such as John Ruskin's *The King of the Golden River* and C.S. Lewis's *Narnia Chronicles*. I study recent books such as the three anthologies collected by the former U.S. Secretary of Education, William J Bennett, *The Book of Virtues,* and Vigen Guroian's *Tending the Heart of Virtue: How Classic Stories Awaken a Child's Moral Imagination.* The best stories for children help them commune with profoundly benevolent laws.

Tales that journey toward positive resolution build strength of soul, and nurture faith and determination to persevere through hard times. They give a reassuring sense of direction to the child-like soul of any age. An imginative scientist who has read all kinds of fairy tales for sixty-seven years said to me recently: 'When I read these old stories, they feel like inoculations of homeopathic snake-venom. They encourage me to go out, live well, and do good!' Stories maintain a stable imaginative space to which you and your children can go again and again to explore different moods of soul. Bruno Bettelheim and other psychologists insist on telling even the most frightening and gruesome classical fairy tales to children, such as *The Juniper Tree*. To meet the challenge of telling them though, it is important to give some time to inner research in a contemplative, objective mood. If you are puzzled or repelled by fairytales, books such as *The Wisdom of Fairy Tales* by Rudolf Meyer and *A Psychiatric Study of Myths and Fairy Tales* by Julius Heuscher may help you understand and deepen your response to them.

The creative content of fairy tales, so intense, compact, and rich with many-layered, resonant pictures, challenges our higher selves. The heightened quality of their language, often too vivid for every day use, sets them apart from ordinary conversation. These stories told by heart, quietly and calmly, allow children to have an experience that might otherwise be unendurable to them. After hearing such wise tales, they will generally rejoice because you have survived the terrible and mysterious events in the tale with them.

Sensitively told, the great fairy tales provide a meditative experience for both teller and listeners. If silence respectfully seals the end of a tale, the deep power of the story goes on weaving. In a long pause, whoever has listened can lengthen and extend their soul space. Much rather than try to explain the meaning of a fairytale, simply tell the story again the next day, and for many days after that. Each time it is told attentively, without a weight of adult emotional response, children gather subtle new resilience through the meaning and understanding they create for themselves.

Some signposts on the way

Children who begin to ask: 'Is this story true?' are able to distinguish a 'story world'. With their imagination they can enter into a story as if they are going to a little theater. When children reach five or six years old, they begin to dream themselves not only into stories from their natural surroundings, but also into classical tales of beggars who become princes, princesses who sleep like death, children who are lost and found again. Seven-year-olds are ready for even very profound transformation stories: the sacred American Indian tale *Jumping Mouse*, or George MacDonald's *The Golden Key*. Much adult 'realism' offends the intelligence of children, who perceive more of life than practical logic. Imaginative tales about humble striving toward magnificence of soul gradually make sense as children become more adept at knowing themselves. Allowed to discover in their own way what the story is about, they actively engage with it, puzzling and prodding to find their own relationship to it. If in the midst of great and mysterious stories, such as the Russian fairy tale, *The Firebird*, they do ask questions, they can be encouraged to find answers for themselves: 'Why do you think the prince fell asleep in the garden?' I like to say firmly to questioning children: 'Let's hear this story again and it will tell us about itself.'

The many virtues deeply instilled into fairy tales lift dark and difficult realities into shining realms. Their 'simpletons' gain love, truth, temperance, justice and power. As test and enchantment met, these tales teach us to expect another test to follow, as waves beat against rock. As one challenge follows another, they help us realize that spiritual companions can come to guard and guide us in our very real daily lives. In *The Three Little Men in the Wood*, the generous child receives generously from the nature spirits in the story. The lazy, selfish girl also receives a true reflection of herself from them. In the sublimely horrendous Grimms' tale *The Juniper Tree,* love and justice ultimately prevail. As Rudolf Meyer and Marie von Franz teach us, vast wisdom resonates in many of these stories. As children listen to the great old tales, such as *Mother Holle* and *Cinderella*, they can become aware of attitudes and behaviors they and others do not always hold. In the modern masterpieces of Maurice Sendak, they learn about fears, jealousy, greed, and laziness that can dominate our better impulses. If frightening tales do not journey to goodness and truth, they leave in a child a residue of increasing fear and helplessness. Stories which leave a child with an aggressive, mean, revengeful or repulsive ending, with no redeeming morality may, it is true, reflect the often harsh and tough game of survival but do not show a way. As Bruno Bettelheim and Julius Heuscher have described at length, in many fairy tales the very mean parent and child are again and again balanced by the very good parent and child, to assure all the family that within us lives the strength, despite any circumstances, to find and give true love.

Imaginative stories of sudden, profound transformation resonate with six and seven-year-old children. Great imaginative tales about humble characters who want to grow toward greater love and goodness can touch their souls deeply. The swift, beautiful, simple language of fairy tales frees them to breathe on a more cosmic level as they go through their deep changes. The spirited little donkey in the Brothers Grimm's story *The Donkey* insists on learning to play music despite the awkwardness of his hooves. In *The Frog Prince* the frog insists on dining with his beautiful though temperamental friend. In *The Waters of Life*, a son learns how to be profoundly helpful to his father. Such great, old, imaginative fairy stories, learned and told in the evening light, enhance the inner life of whoever is fortunate to hear them. A remarkably resilient elder told me recently that his parents, after long workdays, read fairy tales and folk tales to him in the evenings for years. The three of them listened to the stories like wise children together.

When new eagerness to learn awakens in six- and seven-year-olds, they begin to hunger for stories about characters who have sublime goodness and greatness hidden within them. New life pushes into them and their teeth begin to loosen, causing them to feel excitement all the way to their roots. Yet as with so many developmental phases to follow, the joy is accompanied by turmoil and self-doubt. Stories can help children picture the constantly metamorphosing world of which they are a part and reassure them that though they may be awkward for a while, with patience a new phase of life, like new teeth, will emerge. As children, lisping delightfully, experience major structural changes, wise parental words can uncurl a backbone;

strengthen and lengthen shoulder bones; stimulate hands and toes. Teeth and all their developing bones are the foundation of their future individuality. Our patient attention to the quality of words and imaginations that enter a child during these years continues to live in their bones and organs for years to come.

Many parents find that stories with nourishing themes can gradually nudge away less meaningful stories in their household, so that the depth and richness of powerful and wise imaginations echo and resonate. Lesser stories can enter a child's life from many directions, including well-meaning relatives and friends. Weeding these out, like weeding a garden, takes determination and steady effort, so that more truly great stories may sound and resound.

As the imaginations of eight-year-olds take a new direction, the storyteller's style becomes more individual and less dream-like. Having become more sociable, children at this stage test limits and quarrel with one another; they ignore authority figures at times to see how far they can go with their own schemes, projects and resistance to rules and procedures. They are interested in how builders build, bakers bake, policeman uphold law and order. At this age children need swift action and clearly defined characters and morality. Humorous fables and cautionary tales suit eight-year-olds very well, with their clear demarcations of good and bad, showing the result of wise and unwise action. Nine-year-old children become increasingly interested in subversion. They like to turn things upside-down and inside-out, and to enjoy the difference. Jokes and stories with riddles appeal to them. After nine or ten years old, children seek complex plots and down-to-earth characters.

Yet, no matter what their age, children are always drawn towards a respectful, caring and enthusiastic storyteller who radiates kindness, wisdom and enjoyment. The warmth of your storytelling

presence is sacred to your children, sustaining them with calm awareness and confidence as the story unfolds, no matter how disturbed they may feel by some of its words and images. A teacher and grandmother says: 'Just hold the children on your lap and be sure they feel secure and loved. That is the first best place for them to learn to bear what is challenging and frightening.'

Deception or Truth?

Many people equate tales with lying. How can storytelling help children develop a lively relationship with truth? As always, the ways of adults provide primary models for children. They develop a sense for truth from hearing it spoken and from seeing others do as they say. Through our own relationship to what is true they develop theirs. Through our responses, they learn whether honesty is their best policy.

Very young children need much patient help as they learn to know themselves through encounters with many different kinds of reality. A three-year-old gathers all her dolls to give them a tea party and to tell them a story. To her everything is 'real.' Her dolls receive the play of her words and the 'pretend' tea and cakes. Busily, she cares for them, If someone says, 'You had better come and have some *real* tea, she will naturally be bewildered and confused. As parents we can gain skill in gently leading children back and forth across the threshold of their imaginations. 'It is time for your supper with us, and the dolls can enjoy themselves. You have given them a nice tea party.' Our courteous respect for children's imaginative interaction with their playthings and pets, and the stories they create to meet them, helps them to increase their confidence and pleasure in others and their ability to live trustingly with adults.

Because of lies cultivated by the adult world it is surprising that more children do not imitate adult behavior and retreat into fantasy. Fantasy can lead to deceptions and lies, and many children do learn to hide in it for safety. Lies and fantasies attempt to put someone off the truth, so as to solve dilemmas. But as everyone must learn, one lie often leads to another. The most extraordinary adult liar I have met was a confused though oddly pleasant fellow. Throughout his childhood, whatever he said was true had been accepted by his parents, who wanted an accomplished American son. Cleverly presenting the paintings, poems and accomplishments of others as his own, he was a deceptive bundle of 'stories'.

Young children need adults to connect words and objects; words and feelings; words and deeds. The steady clear names of things, people and activities help children to know themselves and one another. Once their sense of language has begun to stabilize, they love to experiment and play with the meaning of words. A mother in a group of parents wrote:

Once there was a clown who thought a bar of soap was a fish. 'That is not a fish,' said the children. But the clown insisted: 'This fish makes bubbles in the water.' 'Those are not fish bubbles. Those are soap bubbles,' the children cried. 'This fish likes to leap out of water,' said the clown. 'That is not a fish coming out of the water. That is soap,' the children shouted. So they decided to give a present to the clown. It was a bar of soap in the shape of a fish. Then both the clown and the children were happy.

As children increasingly enjoy the process of making one thing represent another, they play and pretend more freely. Stories help children find words and pictures to mirror themselves and others: hopping like a rabbit, running like the wind, hiding quiet as a stone. As their inner life and outer capacities unfold, they experience increasingly complex circumstances in picture-language. As they learn to recognize words and images that ring true, when with their playmates they announce, 'We are playing,' they sense there is another state to which they return. By the time they have reached the age of seven or eight, they can fly confidently into metaphors and imaginations that transcend ordinary reality, and 'land' again, knowing that they have been experiencing different kinds of truth. They are able, like the young hero in Michael Ende's *The Never-ending Story*, Dorothy in *The Wizard of Oz*, and the children in C.S. Lewis's *The Lion, The Witch and the Wardrobe*, to explore the borderlands of ordinary adult reality and imagination.

Good storytelling, that reaches children where they are, helps them learn how to distinguish true imagination from mere fantasy. It reveals their deep connection with what lives around and within us, how sunrise and sunset, light and darkness embrace us. Behind imaginations often dwell desires and hopes, fears and doubts that work powerfully in dreams: When we are deeply asleep, impulses and desires produce inner pictures to satisfy us. The stories you tell can play with children's reality, as Maurice Sendak does in his *Night Kitchen* and *Outside Over There*. Storytelling is waking dreaming, moving, quicksilver in the soul, altering reality, like a kaleidoscope; experiences are translated into new meaning, finding the way to a larger sense of reality. True imagination helps children accept, and find pictures and words for all their experiences and feelings.

The difference between truth and lies challenges both children and adults. Some children are impatient with liars in stories; others enjoy 'tall tales' with gusto. Fooling others is a very popular theme in heroic trickster legends throughout the world. Everyone must sooner or later deal with our marvelous human capacity for concealment, distortion, white, grey and darker lies, and how people have lied in order to survive. Yet conscience is a delicate organ that can easily grow askew. The moral of a story can fly over a child's head and leave him with words and pictures he cannot yet connect with moral judgment. A mother told her young son about the first lie she told to her own mother when she was a child: she had tried to explain away a cut in her jacket with: 'The cat did it.' The next day she was surprised when her son cut a jag in his bedspread; she asked how it happened and he earnestly replied, 'The cat did it.' He had not understood the lie.

When children are eight and older they can begin to make practical sense of such classic tales as *The Singing Bone* and *The Boy who Cried Wolf*, cautionary verses such as Hilaire Belloc's *Matilda Who Told Lies*, and the American legends of Paul Bunyan. They can develop vigilant compassion, even for liars.

Refreshing discipline

When you were exposed to painful, disturbing realities, who taught you confidence and gave you a sense of loving protection? The wise disciplinarian is an archetype which can inspire powerful new perspectives. Who cannot benefit from reading *Mary Poppins* by P.L. Travers or *The Wise Woman*, by George MacDonald? Adults in these stories are adept at the exquisite art of discipline; their golden love of children is informed by iron will and diamond-clear thoughts. The parents in these books relinquish their children for a time to these disciplinary geniuses. If you rest from your usual parental role and create such a character, you may find yourself inspired, as I was teaching eight-year-olds. One arduous mid-winter's day I stepped out of the classroom to gather my wits, and when I returned necessity had mothered invention. Mrs. MacIver, a spirited grandmother, had mysteriously arrived to take over my teaching for a time – my imagination had released her full-blown from some secret resource of my soul. This imaginary wizard gave me brilliant new perspectives on the children. She spoke to them with an elderly, robust authority that had come from raising seventeen children back home in Ireland. Both the children I was teaching and my meeker self loved her old-fashioned strictness, her Irish accent and her vivid tales about her grandchildren.

Stories as Birthday Gifts

A six-year-old burst into bitter sobs when her father, who was proud of her scientific interest, gave her a big book for her birthday about insects. She explained indignantly to her parents, still sniffling: 'I wanted to know about insects, but I didn't want to know all that!' When father and mother humbly commune with a child, intuitive wisdom helps them to speak and to give gifts in ways appropriate to their child's real needs.

The gift of a birthday story can help connect children with the mystery and joy of birth. Stories about origins put them in touch with the creative essence at the heart of all that lives. Yet birthday stories can also stimulate questions about aging and death. To celebrate the birthday of their grandmother whose health was failing, a family with young children ranging from three to nine years old invited their friends to have tea and play ordinary children's games with her, such as 'Drop the Clothes-peg in the Bottle.' After their friends had left, the family sat down together to play 'Ask Grandma', a game they made up, during which they were permitted to ask questions freely. The mother wrote out both the children's questions and the grandmother's answers and made them into a gift called 'Grandmother's Birthday Celebration'. The children colorfully decorated the cover and some of the words and sent it, with their granny's permission, to the family members who could not be present.

A birthday can be celebrated with young children for as many days as we have years of age. 'In seventy days grandfather will be seventy years old.' ' In seven days you will be seven years old, and this evening before bed I will give you a story as a gift. Tomorrow someone else in our family will tell your story for you.' Different family members, a favorite doll or puppet telling a story each evening as a birthday approaches, builds a sense of expectation, and of being cherished that grows as the birthday day approaches and in the days following.When the exact day of the birthday arrives, or in the days afterwards, perhaps an older child can be encouraged to tell their own birthday story to the family. Tangible gifts can relate to a story that has been told. A birthday is too precious and vulnerable a time to express in one rampaging party.

Children are greatly influenced by how and when the story of their origin is told. Especially at birthday time, everyone can breathe more freely with a kindly cosmic perspective on our origins, and a sense of continuity with the imponderable ' trails of glory' from which we have come. 'Once upon a time a mother and father were

dreaming of a child…' is a good story to hear. 'An angel saw the dream and went to a child who was longing to come to Earth saying: You will soon be preparing for the journey…'A sense of intelligent cosmic interest, brought out gently and pictorially, allows major questions to sound in the little child. Who am I really? Where did I come from? Who made me? And why am I here on Earth with you? Such a story needs to be heard, perhaps all the more so in troubled circumstances when the relation between parents are strained or the child's situation in other ways is uneasy.

Every great spiritual tradition depicts an archetypal heavenly child who is born to earthly parents. Celestial powers surround all children, which have imbued them with will, feeling and thought, even before earthly conception. If angels seem illusions, our adult 'willing suspension of disbelief' can help children to open a sense of helping guidance from other realms. The saga of *Hiawatha* brings spiritual perspectives in picture and rhymes, for eight year-old children and older, of sublime heroic qualities in the child born to lead and transform several nations. Hiawatha's mother reaches up to receive her child from cosmic heights.

When his daughter was turning four, a hard-working father said, 'I wanted to take more of a part in her life. The process of making a story for her was as much for me as for her.' He started a full month ahead to commune quietly with her, while he was driving through early spring landscapes and weather. On her birthday morning he set a large and a little red chair facing one another with a candle and a bouquet of budding branches on the floor between them. In his story lovely spring buds were opening as a little girl burst out of a house and ran to a swing. 'Push me, push me! She called to her daddy. High! Higher!' As his simple, profound story continued, the girl made a house from cloth and invited her father into it. Beautiful music was coming from meadows and mountains as the little girl sang and played music for him with a dulcimer and bells; he felt he could listen to their music forever. Then the father in the story made a house from a starry cloth 'like a big night sky' and invited the girl into the cosmic house to tell her a story. It was about a girl who wanted to bring the gift of music to the earth.

'I remember the landscape around you when you were born, the stars, and the people. I would like to tell you about them,'another father began very simply. For the first time, he had made a commitment to himself to speak in a special way to his eight-year-old son as his birthday neared. There are many ways to go about reviewing the circumstances of birth. Who was present at the birth? Who else wanted to be there? What were the thoughts of the mother and father as the child was conceived, and gestating, and as it was born? As these facts are shared with loving warmth and carefully chosen words, the child feels reconnected again and again with the early stages of her or his incarnating process. As children mature, more details may be added, giving firm connection to the birth experience as they grow. Later stages of growth repeat in many ways the first birth experience; the many births we experience as we grow are part of the vast world of creation and rebirth, that has sought expression in myth and fairy tale from time immemorial.

The vulnerable time of birthdays is opportune for transforming problems into stories that speak to everyone's deeper listening. I have observed many parents ingeniously helping one another to make imaginative stories as birthday gifts for their young children. Plucking up courage, one of these mothers took the preoccupation of her four-year-old son at his birthday – balancing his new bicycle – and wove it into a bedtime story about a sturdy little oak tree in a storm. A couple concerned about their eight-year-old son's bed-wetting, created an aptly detailed story about the building of a dam. In this story, a giant stole the crucial key to the gate of the dam, but the gatekeeper in due course retrieved it. They kept the story simple and told it in a firm clear voice, without judgment. Another child who had been whooping in quiet places, received a humorous story about a goose, loud of honk, who drank of a quiet green lake and soon could hear the gentle swish of fish and of dragonflies' wings. For her temperamental daughter, a mother's story began: *Once there sat a princess in one corner, and an angry dwarf in another.*

A six-year-old who loved insects was very satisfied with his dad's story about a man who cherished animals, 'and the animal he loved most of all was the caterpillar.'

A giving child received a story about the very young fairy godmother who had a powerful wand of her own.

A ten-year-old who had listened well to many a story, told one for his younger brother as his birthday gift:

A little dwarf cried so loudly that people hurried through his territory. This caused him to wail more loudly, until the trees shook in their roots. At last a little salamander jumped up. 'Why are you crying, little fellow?' And the dwarf said: 'No one will listen to me.' So the salamander said, 'I will stand by you. I will listen to you. I will find what you want. Let us journey through the land together, and if you want to cry, tell me why.

I have enjoyed participating with parents many times in the creation of a story for a birthday party. Since every birthday is a rite of passage, and a vulnerable time for children, when the constellations of their future shine brightly, it is a special opportunity to commune with the direction a child's life is taking. Creating a story which is attuned to a child's needs is like making good bread. Take the finest ingredients you have, mix them in good order, knead them lovingly, adding this and that, then let the bread rise and bake slowly. An aroma lingers after the baking. The nutrients of the story can enter directly into children's life-stream, providing essential elements for growth to strengthen both the listener and the teller.

Suggestions for making birthday stories
When parents want guidance for making birthday stories I offer these suggestions:

1. Desire with all your heart to meet your child's real needs. Your willingness to provide a gift for the child invokes helping protection. In the service of the child's growth, let yourself become a conduit for wisdom to flow through you.

2. Make a time frame, marking the date and hour when you want the story to be ready to share. Give yourself ample time to prepare.

3. With deep respect ponder your child's life. It takes courage to open a very broad outlook on a little child, from conception to maturity.

4. Create a character to represent one or two of your child's strengths. When I am ready to sketch or write out a story, I muse steadily for a few moments until an image of a main character comes to me. I trust this image and, as time permits, paint or draw or describe this character in a few words.

5 Story characters take on a life of their own. The best tales for young children include few descriptive adjectives. They bring their central characters into action from the start and do not psychologize.

6. Commune for a time with a child's problem and allow it to transform into imaginative pictures. The power of imagination clears away more ordinary thoughts so that higher creativity may work and play. Look for an imagination to represent challenges in your children's lives that are developing their character. In wise fairy tales, help for meeting these challenges invariably comes from benevolent and sublime sources.

7. Bring the story to a satisfying and positive conclusion that gives a sense of faith in a loving and lawful world. For young children, no matter what my mood, I make an ending that I hope goes right to the heart of happiness.

A couple decided to create a story for their son who often was disturbing people with sudden boisterous outbursts. In his quiet neighborhood, as his seventh birthday approached, Michael had been racing around climbing trees, shouting wildly for weeks. Yet, he was a good-natured, intelligent boy who was well-liked. His parents sat together with me to conceive a story for his mid-autumn birthday celebration with his teachers and classmates. They sensed that he needed to feel more connected with his father's family, who had been fisher folk in Portugal for many generations; so they decided to set the story in a fishing village in Portugal, where everyone was related to everyone else.

They took turns roughing out the story: the boy's mother carried the thread for a while, then his father. Their desire to create a good gift for him filled them with creativity. Sometimes the story flowed along freely; sometimes eyes closed to find images, their mouths taste-tested words. Using authentic names of the family members felt satisfying. Their story began with colorful imagination:

Among the many islands of the country called Portugal is a little island named San Miguel. Just as the sun arose the color of peaches and paprika, Grandmother Vola opened her eyes and went to feed her chickens and roosters. Grandfather Volo mended his nets. Father Pai strode away to build seaworthy boats. Mother Mai arose to cook her family's breakfast. Jeorg Miguel opened his eyes and stretched. He rushed outdoors to the sunrise when suddenly – through the magnificent colors, he saw a dragon flying.

They wanted their story to express images, language and rhythm to harness Michael's energy and love. Their son had a special friendship with a vulnerable girl in the class whom he protected.

...Olha! Look! Jeorg Miguel went to tell his father in the boatyard and his grandfather in a tangle of nets. He told Vola who was in the henhouse and his Mai who was stirring breakfast gruel. They all came to look as the dragon sped closer. Many children gathered with their parents. Jeorg Miguel took the hand of a little girl, saying quietly and calmly, 'I will take care of this dragon. It will do you no harm.'

Although Michael loved water, he seemed much more interested in fire and air. Suddenly they imagined the boy hurling an old family fishing net into the air. They stayed with this image and the story developed in a surprising way.

Then Jeorg Miguel turned to his grandfather. 'May I use a net today?' At first Volo shook his head. Then in wonder and pride at his grandson, he spread out a freshly mended net. Jeorg rolled it together, slung it over his shoulders proudly, and secured it around his waist, as he had seen his grandfather do many times. Very carefully, with his heavy load on his back, the boy began a long climb and at last he reached the top of a tall tree. There he sat and rested; leaves covered his head. In his hiding place he planned what he would do. He could see the dragon descending upon the empty schoolyard. Gathering his strength, Miguel stood and pushed his head out from the top of the tree. As the dragon hurtled toward him he tilted back his head and yelled continuously and loudly, his tongue vibrating all the way to the back of his throat. On the third throw of his grandfather's net, the boy sent it out in a full sweep and caught the dragon – a wildly bellowing tangle of sharp wings and claws. Miguel held on with all his might and gathered the net into a sack. The dragon struggled and spat and kicked and thrashed, but the boy managed to land it in a heap in the schoolyard, where the people of the island built a cage for it.

The story ended:

Some say the dragon gave its fire to help the children learn and grow. Some say it returned to the stars over the oceans. The people of San Miguel remember Miguel and his dragon. And to this day on the island children yell like Miguel did at the top of the tree and leave the dragon-cage door open.

After the story Michael's father taught the children a Portuguese fishing song with a loud chorus that he remembered from his own childhood. The family sang the song and shared the story repeatedly, bringing the boy closer to his Portuguese ancestry at a sensitive time in his development. The story had given them new perspective, without criticism, on the growing power of the boy's voice.

Death and Transformation

Children are very close to death because they are so close to birth. They carry a natural wisdom. 'If they haven't died yet, they are living still,' end many of the old tales. Stories give a long perspective. Recently I made a little story for a child who had begun to feel anxious about his grandfather's growing fragility.

'Who are you?' asked the little fox? The old man said, 'I came long ago from the stars. My mother bore me and blessed me. My father blessed me too and made for me a little rocking cradle. I lived with them for a long time in a little house. They sang to me and told me stories until I grew into a boy. Then that boy became a man. And here you see me now, gray as an owl, getting ready to fly back to the stars. 'Stay,' said the little fox,' and we can play together.' 'Thank you,' said the old man, 'because you have asked me, I will stay a while longer.' So the old man and the fox played and children came, and so did their parents and friends, and one day they held a great feast because it was the birthday of the child who came from the stars to become a man.

Stories can create broad perspectives when they are needed: a sense of balance and order in times of anxiety. Preparation comes in many ways for major transitions, including death. A friend of a mother who could not attend her grandmother's funeral in a distant land, recently made a story for her and for her children.

Once there was a girl who loved to swim. It was as if she had been born in the water. One day as she swam the girl saw a shimmering silver starfish. She dived but could not reach it, so she swam strongly up and then to the shore to rest. The next time she dove deeper. The third time her starfish was gone! She swam in circles in panic. Every day she returned to see if it was there. At last she looked – and there was the starfish on the beach. She took it to the ocean's edge and set it free.

Another mother remembered with her children the entire life of their pet rabbit, Carrot-stick. Soon after it died they made a memory book together, which the mother helped them to illustrate. The first two chapters were about the birth of the little rabbit. Chapter Three was entitled 'Much Older'; Chapter Four, 'Much, Much Older'; Chapter Six was entitled 'Death', Chapter Seven 'Funeral.' The mother created the time frame and wrote out the story as the children shared their memories. Each of the children lovingly illustrated the book.

One spring day a family with four children saw a herring gull that had been hit by a golf ball fall into a small pond. Dozens of other gulls gathered overhead, crying to the wounded gull. The family was unable to help the gull. After it died the children waited as the wind pushed it to the shore. Their parents helped the children lift it out of the water and bury it in the hollow of a tree. Singing a song they had sung at other impromptu funerals for animals they found, they covered the bird with leaves and flowers. Then they made up stories about what the bird had seen and done during its lifetime.

When they returned home they wrote a poem together. The mother helped the children find words to describe this upsetting, exciting and awe-inspiring experience. Their mother shared with me the book they created. Each page is a large watercolor painting on which the story is written in verse with colored pencils. The work of illustration was divided among them; the eldest wrote out the finished story-poem. For several weeks after that the children wanted to hear it and to remember the beautiful bird.

A sea gull falling from the sky,
A snow white beauty from on high,
Plummeted into Blacknook Pond,
Injured by the golfer's wand.

Down around the shore so near
Children watch with awe and fear.

With flapping wings and struggling head
It twists and turns until it's dead.
Grief fells the onlooker's hearts
When a life on earth departs.

Fellow seagulls circle round –
Call their brother on the ground.
He answers not the desperate sound.
The earth is silent all around.

On the water, still afloat,
Soft winds push the light bird boat.
On the opposite shore he lands
Into loving outstretched hands.

On closer look the children see
The glory of the gull of sea.
Struck by the beauty of his beak
And soft feathers, white and sleek.

Wings that carried him o'er the sky
Now lifeless in their splendor lie.
A palanquin of sticks for the snow-white king.
A song to Mother Earth we'll sing.

We'll carry him to the hollow tree
A tomb of nature it will be.

Dandelions, leaves, gill-over-the-ground,
Celandine, forsythia, adorn the mound.

A door of branches we shall weave
In guarded peace the gull to leave.

The spirit of this bird lives on
In every sea gull's flight and song.

Their creative storytelling helped them to find unusual strength as a family in many other situations.

The grief and anxiety that even very resilient children feel as they experience changes in people and things around them can surprise us. Especially children who have experienced the death of a sibling or parent or friend, can feel overwhelmed for a long time by their instinct to mourn. Like an underground stream, tears may go deep, or burst out as torrential wailing. Between the extremes live many varieties of sorrow, sometimes accompanied by anger or rage. All these emotions can be mirrored in stories.

A mother was distraught at the piteous crying of her five-year-old, her only daughter, who had been abandoned by her father at birth. Together we found a story imagination to help them both gain perspective on their loss, especially at bedtime:

Once there was a little house, which by night became a huge mansion. In this mansion were many rooms. In one of the rooms, at the end of a very long corridor, was a shining pool. When the big door closed upon this pool, whoever was inside felt safe.

This pool was filled completely with tears that had been cried over many years. These had been given by fathers and mothers, grandparents, great uncles and aunts and newborn babies and children. The salty water kept afloat people who could not even swim. At times this pool of accumulated tears seemed as big as an ocean.

When the people who lived in the mansion wanted to cry they went to the room of the magical pool; whoever left this room could return. The pool kept all their tears. Whoever swam there could stay afloat for a long time. When all their tears had been cried, they would climb out of the pool and wrap themselves in a beautiful blanket. Then they would fall softly asleep, and awake joyful, peaceful and refreshed.

Stories can bring forth the sometimes unexpected wisdom and sensitivity of children towards death. When her infant brother died unexpectedly, an eight-year-old girl asked me to read her a beloved story she had heard a few months previously. In *The Golden Key*, by George MacDonald, two children find their way to a rainbow which leads them into the deepest mysteries of death and birth. She painted a series of radiant rainbow bridges to help her brother on his way. Her pictures inspired her friends, who asked that their rainbow bridges also be buried with the baby.

Moving

Changing houses is unsettling for everyone, yet the power of imagination can enfold this time and sooth tempers and upsets. Resting amidst packing boxes before lunch or before sleep is an opportunity for storytelling. In preparation for a move, children can hold and wonder at the carrying power of a seed whose outer shell, like a minuscule moving van or tiny packing box, conceals the power to manifest again in a new place. Each person, during a move, like a seed, carries the capacity to make a new life. Noah and his family preparing for their voyage is a mighty picture of moving onward. The ship, itself a seed, carried on the ocean what was needed to start again. Early settlers in America, depicted in Laura Ingalls Wilder's books, demonstrated this capacity to build a good life in strange surroundings.

A family with three young children was about to move in late summer from town to a village by the sea. Their mother told them quietly about bees swarming because the farmer needed the place where they had lived. Another day she spoke about a flock of geese that were content where they lived, yet when they heard other geese calling overhead their hearts stirred. They rose and circled their pond, looking down on their favorite places, until one fine day with a great surge they set out for new lands.

A child of five was crying while sleepwalking every night, after he moved with his family to a new part of the city. When his distressed mother came to see me, we made up a story for her to tell at bedtime. It was about an old house. In the story the old house sags and creaks when the family moves. But, as the new family arrives with shouts of happiness, and warm cooking smells rise from the kitchen stove, the house becomes comforted and holds the new family in its 'arms'. The story worked like a charm.

If you are moving soon, you might make a book cut in the shape of a house. As you turn the pages write a blessing of appreciation for each of its rooms. Just before your final departure you might go through the house describing the function of each room, with wonder and gratitude, and encircle the house, perhaps with colorful flags, singing good-byes to the whole house and its surroundings. Especially for the children you might tell the story of a house's feelings as a new family and pets arrive, or as you are settling in to your new place, speak directly to it and tell it about your former home.

Storytelling in Sickness

When children who are ill must let go of their usual enjoyments, quiet down, and rest, stories offered by a devoted storyteller can be like gates through which healing light streams. During these times children are in a highly creative state and need to feel themselves surrounded by adults who are peacefully creative and confident: they are especially influenced by adult attitudes. An ongoing story can help both parents and children during this time.

A mother told a story about a spider as she held her daughter through many hours of high fever. Her daughter insisted the story keep on spinning; even as she dozed in her mother's arms she wanted to hear her telling the story, humming and singing more of the spider's adventures. The mother did not know where the image had come from. In the story, a mother spider watched over a little spider. Trees, crickets and other creatures sang to her. The wind was sometimes friendly and sometimes broke the threads of the web, and she would have to start her spinning again. The healing power of this imaginative story and its gentle spider wisdom lasted several hours, and held them both, while the deep frightening fever process continued and finally broke. The mother was amazed at how the story kept telling itself through her, and how beautiful her voice became as she gave herself completely to her child through it.

Another mother discovered how to help her five-year-old son get well by becoming his personal storyteller. Five years of living with his asthma, inherited from both sides of his family, were wearing her down. Many zealous friends were further exhausting her with their ideas about what might help him. Convinced that she must protect him, she was relieved and excited to realize that she herself could create story medicine. With a little encouragement, this mother began trusting her imagination, even during her son's full-blown asthma attacks. After a succession of sleepless nights, one early spring morning on the verge of driving their son again to the hospital, her husband suggested, 'Maybe it's time for a story.' The exhausted mother looked at her husband, and took a deep breath. As the first of her stories ended, the boy's breathing had changed; he was able soon afterwards to go to sleep. Prior to this discovery, night after sleepless night, she and her husband had distracted their son with storybooks. Later she said: 'In my experience, reading a book did not heal because it was not enough of a present time experience. Each crisis is a very present tense experience that includes John's entire universe.'

Dragons became helpful story entities for this family because dragon breath pours out powerfully, unlike the out-breath that is so challenging for asthmatics:

Once there was a fire so enormous it attracted the attention of every dragon in the land. The King of the dragons told the baby dragon to stay home where it was safe, but the little dragon followed his father. When the dragons came together he was clever enough to stay hidden, yet he could see and hear everything.

The story proceeded with the special inspiration that can be found by parents under pressure.

The mother had decided to be open to receive even very surprising and intricate imagery as the story evolved. After experiencing the bizarre alchemical dream-story of a glass tulip that did not give up its fire, carried by giants in the middle of the night, their son painted pictures of fiery breath. He filled their house with dozens of pictures, became 'clear' and slept well soon after.

Another series of made-up stories served them about a boy who loved dogs but was allergic to them, and a dog named Richard Robertson, who made many animal friends. These stories often seemed extraordinary, incomprehensible events. The mother said: 'Through years of sleeplessness I feel the most important thing I am doing during these stories, and the drawing or painting he does afterwards, is to protect the space psychically. Allergy draws many kinds of forces. I invoke the highest Spirit. I tell a story and I pray without ceasing all at the same time.'

This mother believes that her son survived his earlier years through the stories that they wove together, and the paintings and drawings he made at all hours of the day and night to discharge, contain and embody them. In a similar way to the mother struggling with her child's asthma, you might create a story about a dragon who can bellow radiant colors, music, flowers or jewels.

A father whose young daughter was suffering from leukemia fainted during her painful medical tests. Eventually he and his wife learned how they could participate in her healing by becoming remarkable storytellers. The side effects of the chemotherapy had heightened all the child's senses so the touch of sheets on her skin and food in her mouth were sometimes excruciating. Stories helped her relax and release her pain. In desperation one night, because an old bedtime reading ritual would not put her to sleep, the father had turned off the light and began to tell her a story. In a few minutes in the dark, with his voice sounding gently around her, she was asleep. He started with stories he could remember, *Goldilocks* and *The Three Bears*, *Little Red Riding Hood*, *The Three Pigs*, and after telling these every night, they both tired of them and he began to improvise.

Soon they started to make up their own imaginary stories. 'What a wonderful quiet adventure it was. We would start with an outdoor setting which both of us knew, like the cottage we visited during the summer. I would describe the scene for us with sights, sounds, and smells of a warm summer day. From there, anything could happen. We would imagine her pulling a star out of her pocket, holding it tight, and making a wish. Pegasus would take Elizabeth for a ride on a rainbow around the lake. She could transform herself endlessly into a mermaid, a dolphin – any animal she wanted.' After three years of chemotherapy, with her health improved, she resisted the treatments more and more vigorously. Yet she continued to relax into stories throughout the sometimes very painful healing process. Her father, still modest and self-conscious as a storyteller, would pluck up his courage and say, 'I'll tell you a story.' 'Ok, let's go,' she would reply. After screaming a little when the nurse pulled the marrow, she would say with determination, 'Go on, finish it!' In the end her health returned.

An assortment of colored cloths can stimulate the story process. They can be arranged on the bedclothes, on a warm carpet in the child's room or in another part of the house where they will not be disturbed. As you and your child's imagination shape the cloths into cave, mountain, valley, life forces are stirred by a subtle, colorful flow of colors and images. Simple representations of larger realities leave the children free to play in their own way. Ornate dolls and toys tend to leave no soul space for children's own activity and so do not stimulate healing imagination. A stone can become a farmhouse; a postage stamp a postman; a pillow a heavy cloud; a feather an angel. Children can play quietly for a long time in a creative space that gently surrounds and holds them, seated amidst the colors as if in a healing dream. Left free to develop their own story, images of plants, animals, earth spirits, angels will arise naturally to help them heal and grow.

During health emergencies, tape recordings and videos of family members reading stories can occasionally be a gift. Although electronic communication usually distances the child from us, however acoustically refined or filled with fine speech and tales, yet when my eldest brother was gravely ill, his wife suggested that he tape-record stories for his grandchildren, who lived hundreds of miles away. She first selected *The Velveteen Rabbit* by Marjorie Williams, a sensitive story about loss and death for young children. When his voice and the book arrived, my nephew and his wife sat with their young sons, who were not yet ready to read, teaching them to coordinate the pages and pictures with the words, linking warmth across the generations. The love my brother was able to express to them all through the story was an important step in his recovery.

5 Storytelling Through the Seasons

The seasons form a great circle in their changing.
Black Elk

*You yourself are another little world and have within you
the Sun, the Moon and Stars.*
Origen

Autumn Stories

Whenever we humbly open our senses with little children to the natural world, inspiration streams toward us. Many traditional stories affirm that nature speaks to us all – and that we are dependent on her wisdom. From time immemorial children have sensed secrets hidden in natural forms. An American Indian tale portrays a boy who listens carefully to a wise old rock to receive its ancient secrets. He becomes a custodian of all the rock has told him and is able to strengthen his village. In the Germanic fairy tale, *The Queen Bee*, a simpleton protects the lives of ants, ducks and bees and as a result saves many human lives.

Two small children found a leaf on their path on their daily walk through a summer park with their mother. In a twinkling it became for them an imaginary friend, who agreed to come home in one of their pockets. The mother was surprised to see how happily the children played, introducing him to their toys. While the children slept, this mother, inspired by their relationship with what was more than a leaf, found herself making a little book full of colorful crayon drawings of the leaf man and the children, surrounded by stars, sun and moon. She sewed its pages together with a pliable green twig. In the morning the children found the book, just the size of the leaf, at their bedside waiting to be read. 'The leaf man told me this story,' she said, ' and I drew it for you.' They listened to the very simple story she had written with complete joy and attention.

In the weeks and months that followed other characters came to life for this family through a combination of observation and imagination - a bark family, a rock family. A stone that held rainwater spoke. One day some flowers became simple puppets. The children soon had the knack of playing with these puppets and entertained her with spontaneous little puppet stories performed outdoors from behind a tree root, or in their living room at home. Wind, sunbeams, and a variety of insects and birds shared the stage. Sometimes in the evenings before they fell asleep, she or her husband retold the stories they had made up.

Through all the seasons, children can be encouraged to experience Earth as a living presence full of wisdom and love. When it is time to tell a story, a place at home devoted to the Earth will take on increasing significance from the stories told there. With her three-year-old daughter, a mother created a corner called Mother Earth's Garden. Together they brought natural objects to it that had drawn their attention. Every evening before sleep the mother helped her daughter remember through caring words and little songs what they had collected there. Because she wanted her daughter to love all the seasons with her, one gray day of sleet and ice the mother began to sew story capes for herself and her daughter, to wrap themselves closely and symbolically in the life-body of nature. On one side of the capes she embroidered small spring and summer flowers and butterflies they had observed carefully together. On the other, she placed small autumn leaves cut out of felt – a scurrying spider, flying birds and snowflakes. When the flowers were visible on the outside, signs of colder seasons were concealed. When the snowflakes embroidered on the shoulders of the capes appeared, the flowers were hidden invisibly, near their hearts.

As late summer sees the disappearance of green on a vast scale, the energies of transformation awaken a desire to collect and store things away. It is the perfect time to gather stories that are appropriate for autumn. Dogs and other creatures begin to create their winter coats, and a longing for warm clothes and stories comes over us. Children feel this instinctively, although many are one or two generations removed from the traditional canning and preserving of fruit and vegetables that used to happen in homes everywhere.

Stories such as *The Three Little Pigs* can creatively embody the foreboding and growing excitement felt by adults and children at the approach of autumn. Though some children revel in it, many worry about the tremendous destructive power in the natural world; yet when our stories convey natural wisdom, children around us can grow in wonder at the ineffable mothering power that surrounds us. Mother Nature knows how to help everything that dies, tending her multitudes of seeds and winter-hearty buds. With infinite capacity, she receives innumerable offerings of old flower petals, dead moths and bees, and takes them into her houses of transformation. She can be portrayed, with her assistants, singing and telling stories about rest, and preparations to grow anew.

One autumn when I was a young woman, a kindergarten teacher asked me to be Mother Nature for her class. Several parents dressed me ceremoniously in a long brown robe and tucked leaves and long grasses gracefully into the hood as hair. With casual bravado, as I surrendered to this role, I soon found myself enthroned majestically in front of the children – surrounded by fruits and nuts in beautiful bowls and huge bunches of sunflowers and chrysanthemums, some of them faded and drooping. As I suddenly came to inhabit this vast and sacred archetype, I found myself large beyond measure while each child stepped forward to present me with something to take care of for the winter – seeds, a dead bee and moth, a spider's egg, and old flower petals they had warmed with their hands. I placed each of their offerings, slowly and carefully, in my silk pouches, searching far beyond and within me to find a voice powerful and loving enough to express the ineffable magnitude I felt. As the ceremony ended, it was all I could do to intone a blessing. I moved with unfamiliar grandeur out the door of the classroom and wandered about for a long time afterwards, hoping I might return to my customary self, and survive the immensity of the wisdom I felt from communing in this way, so unexpectedly, with the Great Mother.

Many other traditional story figures uphold autumn's mysteries. Shape-shifters, they sometimes appear in the form of old people or children who have strength and light enough to shine through death. Where such fearful mysteries lurk, they transform darkness into good. The Archangel Michael is one such figure, represented in many a holy icon and place of worship – a timeless hero often shown riding into the chaos of autumn on a huge steed, carrying with him a sword of light. Spirit Master of this ominous season, he finds dragons of cruelty and greed wherever they are. When he has slain them then he inspires people to speak wisely with a potion of dragon tongue. With essence of dragon tooth and bone, he strengthens fields to bring forth good crops in the spring. With dragon scales, he makes sharp instruments for the creation of beautiful things. Sometimes, he gives children strength, in hard and dangerous times, to save themselves and their whole world; his guiding presence teaches them what is hidden in seeds and how, in sharpest killing cold, they and their families and communities can survive.

Autumn is a natural time to ask children what they want to become when they grow up and to weave their dreams into stories. It is also a time to remember saints and saintly aspects of family members whose good deeds shine, like light in the midst of darkness. Such stories prepare for winter, just as pumpkins are smiling suns in the wasteland of a shriveled garden. As plants die at the change of season, children are naturally sensitive to the mystery of death, although they may not yet know how to speak of it. A story can help them feel part of a large and lawful cosmos. A thoughtful mother I know created a group of acorn fairies one autumn, whose heads were shiny acorns. Around each head she sewed a little body and a jaunty green hat. She told her children that these little ones carried in their heads splendid oak trees, which would emerge in an unknown future.

I once was asked by the parents of a boy becoming six years old in late October to help them make a story for his birthday. At the time they were both distressed because he had been attacking his three-year-old sister mercilessly with words and throwing things. He wanted only one thing for his birthday – a sword. His parents and I met and thought deeply together about their child, his fiery aggressive energy, and his otherwise earnest sweetness. We wanted to make a tactful story to honor his mettle and spirit and also help him to calm down. As we let our imaginations work together we eventually created a character that represented the complexities of his personality – a prince who lived in a castle, the proud owner of many horses. As our story evolved, the prince led a wild life there – until one day he was painfully thrown from his favorite roan. Then a powerful magician arrived mysteriously, astride a huge white steed. Eventually, in our story, the prince was found worthy to receive from this magician a magical sword, together with instructions for its use. At the magician's command, the prince agreed before using his sword to say specific words, and to learn them by heart. The mother made a simple tune to accompany the magician's words: *Brave and true will I be/ Each kind word sets me free/ Each good thought makes me strong/ I will fight for the right; I will banish the wrong.* At the birthday party I told the story of the prince and his new sword, singing the verse three times. Then the parents, in a slow-paced ceremony, presented their son with a wooden sword, that had been lovingly carved by a friend. At the tip of the sword, the boy's parents had placed a shining candle in a candle-holder. Other evenings, when the candle-sword had been lit, the mother and sometimes the father too, retold our story and sang the song

with their son. Eventually it streamed through them all, body and soul. For many months a fiery sequence of stories followed about the prince and his red horses, in which the prince endeavored always to keep his promise to the magician, but often forgot. The mother, son and all the family revered the sword, which was suspended, like a vision, in mid-air over the child's bed. The story brought an enduring and benevolent balance to the whole family.

Autumn's vigorous bounty invites gratitude. When parents gathered to make stories around this theme for mealtimes, one mother began: *Once upon a time children in the land called Mesopotamia looked for the Big Dipper every evening before dipping their spoons into their family soup pot.* A couple requested help from the group because their four-year-old had piteously wailed as they brought the traditional roasted turkey to the table at Thanksgiving time in America. In a small and tearful voice, he had confessed to them, 'I wanted to play with it!' The parents were stunned and perplexed. The group put their hearts together to contemplate native peoples of the earth who are open and sensitive to the creatures upon which they feed and depend. Gradually they created a story about an

Indian tribe who loved wild turkeys, protected them and prayed for them. A little boy who lived in the village was asked by a wise man of the tribe to live with the wild turkeys, and learn their ways. The Indian boy practiced until the Celebration Day, when he danced for the whole tribe with the strong and proud turkey spirit all around him. The next year at Thanksgiving time, the boy danced with his father a turkey dance that deeply touched the whole family. His mother added more food choices to the traditional turkey dinner.

Children often seek stories to express and dispel their fears. A king or a dragon in a story may shout: *If you don't do as I say, I will eat you all.* Fear of being eaten lurks at the core of every 'little muffin', as children are sometimes affectionately called. Only slowly does the human mouth learn to defend itself with words, to insist, 'I am not a muffin. I am your child.' Beginning with very simple tales for young children about the vast cooperative endeavor in which we live with our natural surroundings, a good story can portray how a song nourishes a tree; a fish nourishes a bear, a prayer an angel. For generations classics such as The *Gingerbread Man* and *Little Red Riding Hood* have given young children perspective on their desires and appetites.

With the help of other storytelling parents, an overly anxious mother was able to make up a story for her six-year-old, who with both dread and exhilaration, had lost his two front teeth:

Once there was a comfortable little hill of boulders and stones. One night just as summer was ending, there came a big storm. The wind rolled noisily and pushed on and on at the hill. At last, the biggest boulder fell down into a stream. Another followed it. The wind whistled in the open places where the rocks had been. A young shepherd came with his bright white sheep, who loved the whistling wind. He built a strong new house in the empty places.

Because her sensitive son wanted to hear this story repeated several times, she was inspired to find other events in the natural world to provide reassuring pictures for him during the seasonal changes ahead. Because he enjoyed hearing about children very like himself, she soon made another story of a boy who loved eating bread. In the story, an ogress dressed in black moved into the village where he lived, blowing out all the oven fires in the village and throwing away the people's baking tins, like leaves, into the river. But an old farmer and his wife who lived outside the village took the boy in and taught him the secrets of leaven. As he helped the old ones with threshing, separating out kernels from the shafts of grain, and turning a stone wheel to grind grain into soft flour, these tasks awakened understanding of the continuity that exists among all things. He baked truth into the bread in their oven, and brought it to the villagers – all who ate it became strong enough to drive the ogress out.

The boy, who had often been afraid of the dark, liked this story and wanted to hear it many times. He asked his mother if she would put a reassuring, freshly-baked bun under his pillow as he slept at night to remind him of it. Their acceptance of the inevitable and meaningful nature of change allowed them both a unique kind of happiness.

You might gather seeds with your children and place them in a protected place. Ask the child to tell you a story about a seed. Where does it like to sleep? Who watches over it as it sleeps? Why is the marigold seed different from the nasturtium seed? As you listen carefully to their stories, they may inspire your own.

The mysteries of nourishment are a continual theme for children. The Tomten, described by Astrid Lindgrun in several books, represents elemental nature's interest in food that has been offered to it with loving human respect. In *The Golden Key* by George

MacDonald, an ethereal flying fish leaps willingly into a cooking pot for a child who is prepared to receive it. A grandmother with spiritual insight told her grandchildren about the hunger of angels, saying that they come very eagerly to be nourished at mealtimes by the conversations of human families. The children asked her to tell them what angels do when they receive a good meal. This began a series of absorbing tales about the interweaving of angelic and human lives.

Winter Stories – Storytelling with the Stars

In northern climes, winter brings a sense of eternity, and of patient renewal. Children communing with its darkness and stillness sense invisible guardians watching over their lives and stars as shining friends. Especially in the evenings, it is important to create warmth and quiet for children to contemplate for themselves distant worlds, when a sense of wheeling order in the starry dome above can give calm guidance. Although the mysteries of children's inner life are a private domain, as they fall asleep they can be reassured by stories of real birds, whales, butterflies and other creatures which, when lost or separated, like sailors and pilots, orient themselves by the stars.

Story time in the midst of dark winter can coax the courage of young children to grow, inspiring them with confidence that they too can live to tell even the most desperately chilling adventures. As Bruno Bettelheim frequently insists in *The Uses of Enchantment*, frightening stories are necessary food for children to develop essential resources and mettle for life. They are best absorbed by children when spoken by a wise adult who remains calmly loving and confident before, during and after sharing the terrible tale.

Around age seven many children begin to feel loyalty toward their family and friends. Especially when bright and lovely outer forms fall away in winter, its warmth shines. A multitude of fairy tales and much of the best fantasy literature revolve around this theme. In *The Two Brothers,* when the siblings part, a dagger driven into a tree tells of their safety or danger. In *The Princess and the Goblin* by George MacDonald, after the princess has climbed many flights of stairs and entered a strange upper room, she discovers a beautiful old lady, unfailingly spinning threads of wisdom to guide her way. At first the child is disappointed in her gift because she cannot see the thread, but she soon discovers its ineffable power.

Many classic fairy tales in a wintry mood support the deepest morality of our human souls. In *The Wolf and The Seven Little Kids,* when the kids are left to fend for themselves by their mother, six of them are consumed by the wolf that enters the house. The smallest one, who jumps into the clock, is quick to help its mother when she returns, like springtime, to bring the others back to life out of the wolf's belly.

Sunlit frost covered the windows one midwinter, as I joined a circle of children while a storyteller slowly lit a candle. Like countless storytellers with an eager and trusting audience of children, necessity bestowed grace to her voice. She sang and spoke a story about a snow fairy whose wings during an ice storm had caught on a thornbush. The others had flown on, leaving the tiny snow fairy behind. At last her cries for help were heard by a large-eared elf, who sang his way to her through the tangled underbrush, and brought her to the safety of his healing hut and crystal potions and salves. The children blissfully joined in with her simple spontaneous melodies that represented the voices of the storm, the snow fairy, and of the kindly elf who helped her wings to heal.

Winter is a natural time to practice singing and making music together: pure tones can surround us like snowflakes. I recently

watched a five-year-old place music upside down on a piano, as she prepared to create a little story song for the whole world. Angels seemed to guide her voice and the piano notes, as together they flew effortlessly up and down like birds.

Yet we adults are often resistant to singing. A mother who believed she could not sing a note in tune, nevertheless wanted to take part in a winter puppet presentation of an old Rumanian tale. In the story a maiden lives for seven years with an enchanted bear, until her love transforms him into the true prince he was. For many personal reasons, she wanted to play the part of the maiden. Yet in spite of our whispers, 'You *can* sing', in all the rehearsals, she insisted that someone else sing the maiden's songs. On the day of our first performance, the musicians arrived, taking considerable time and pleasure warming up their instruments. Finally the room darkened, and as the curtain rose to the clear tones of their little overture, the woman was astounded to feel herself moving gently through a sound barrier. Suddenly, perfectly in tune, her voice sang in a clear stream – she continued to sing in tune throughout the puppet show. Strangely, still convinced that she could not sing, she afterward denied all the clear music that had poured beautifully through her.

At winter solstice, the turning point of the year when new light begins to penetrate darkness, it is helpful for children to receive stories of birth told simply and respectfully. As they hear of the many gifts newborn children everywhere receive from earth and beyond, they can imagine love pouring like sunlight and starlight to even the most neglected children. *Star Child*, a haunting story from the Grimms' collection, portrays a child of wintry purity. As the child journeys she gives away all her possessions; yet, in exchange for her willing generosity, she receives a new life, full of blessings. Within religious writings live themes which can profoundly stimulate our own story-making, whatever our background may be. Many families read scriptural stories again and again until the whole family knows every word. Traditional religions can inspire transcendent storytelling; tales from the childhood of Buddha and Krishna and the Christian story of the birth of Jesus portray many archetypal situations. Those who traveled great distances to find these divine infants are like parents seeking to share their best with their children. A childlike soul within all of us responds to the shepherds in the traditional Christian story, who only find the new-born child through celestial guidance. Cold rejection of the devoted young couple, the child who is threatened by the envious king, are pictures which speak to everyone's personal life. The very young and oldest among us rejoice to hear that when we are tired and downcast, we can be uplifted by angels.

A well-known Italian story, *Old Befana*, portrays an old woman who dies, and runs breathlessly through the stars. According to the story, which is told in different versions in several countries, she descends at mid-winter in search of the pure spirit in every child. Wherever she visits she leaves behind her a sacred sense of starlight, a well-swept house, and sweet gifts. I once attended a party during which adults and children lay down in a warm candle-lit room to hear Old Befana's story. 'Please relax, close your eyes, and keep them closed through the whole story,' said the storyteller with a warm, commanding voice. The sound and sweet scents of a real-life Befana sweeping gently and vigorously through the room blended with his words at intervals throughout the story. When the story finished and all was still, we opened our eyes to find star-shaped treats had been laid upon our hearts. You too might learn to tell a version of this story to share with your children, or freely imagine another different sublime visitor who sees deeply into the lives of children and helps them to grow.

Winter is a perfect time to collect fairytales about the search for warmth and wisdom of love. St. Valentine's Day in mid-February brings another timely opportunity for telling tales which banish fears, and enliven our hearts. The Christian Lenten season evokes humility and inspires kinder and more noble expression. I am often moved during this season to tell a traditional Irish legend, about the power of the fairies to transform lives. The hero of the tale *Lusmore,* a basketweaver, humbly adds his voice to the moonlit singing of fairies; and they, in return, magically remove the hump from his back. And like innumerable other such fairy tales, folk tales and fables from around the world, this tale too contains a weak character who lacks Lusmore's generosity of heart, and ends up with a bigger burden than he had at the start. Because such characters do not share humbly and generously with others, they suffer enchantment, so that they may grow more wise.

The gradual return of the light stimulates new growth in multitudinous forms. As roots of indoor plants deepen in their pots, in the night of late winter, children's internal organs grow; their bones elongate. Late winter is a good time to hold children in our laps, when they are not too large, to breathe gently and reassuringly, and to shape houses out of warm coverlets in which, as we tell stories with them, we too can feel cozy and safe, to begin new growth.

Spring Stories

As new growth unfurls in spring, adults naturally ponder the unfathomable immensity that lives condensed in little children. In early spring, a mother found a cloth covered with subtle stars and pinned it onto walls and ceiling to form a canopy over her six-year-old daughter's bed. Each evening, the radiant star-cloth quietly enclosed their story space. During her daughter's early growing awareness of her own place in creation, mother and daughter were both deeply contented by simple tales about the nest-building activities of birds and beavers and other such creatures who bear within them sublimely invisible patterns. The mother said, 'I spoke quietly with the stars when I told stories during these sensitive times – I was careful not to break her mood of contemplation. My daughter would gather all her dolls around her like companions from far and near and liked to sit very still with them, her eyes open and dreaming.' Communing deeply with her daughter, she said that certain words and images seemed to fly rapturously to them, like celestial birds.

As birds flew into their garden one spring, a father who had studied American Indian wisdom wanted his children to experience their unique spirit, and share his loving interest in birds, trees and flowers. Watching in his garden, he studied their qualities and behavior. The children often came to him with questions, which he sometimes answered by reading a story from native American lore, perhaps by Joseph Bruchac or Medicine Bear; or he would tell a story about what was happening right before their eyes.

Another father experienced difficulty telling nature stories to both of his children at the same time. He had read *The Wonderful Adventures of Nils* by Selma Lagerlof when he was a boy, and had taken great pleasure imagining himself riding over vast miles, like

Nils on the back of a wise and friendly bird. Yet when the return of birds in flocks awakened the thoughtful questions of his eight-year-old son, he sensed this was not yet the right story for him. 'Which bird is really leading them?' asked the boy earnestly. 'Do the leaders change? Or is the flock like one great bird?' His son wanted plain, straight-forward answers to these questions. He especially wanted to know about unwise leaders. *The Emperor's New Clothes* was his favorite story. But his six-year-old sister preferred thoroughly imaginative tales, such as *Jorinda and Joringel*, about a girl who was turned into a bird for a time by a wicked witch. The father wanted to tell stories to content both his children at the same time. To his relief, he discovered *The Firebird*, a mystical Russian tale about a phoenix with feathers like the rising sun, which deeply pleased them all.

In spring, all our senses meet the beauty and nobility of our earth, but to speak of it calls for imagination. A down-to-earth mother who wanted to tell stories to her young children felt dull and silly whenever she tried to launch into imaginative pictures. Yet with the encouragement of others, she decided to risk describing spring to them personified as a queenly lady. Her children had heard about Lady Spring at school and willingly brought her into their playtime imaginations at home. As if intentionally to reassure their mother, one sunlit morning they invited the archetypal lady to their breakfast table, having decorated her place with little buds and leaves. The children were sure that Lady Spring did not need to eat anything and had never experienced any season but spring. They took turns to have a fiery little dragon on a box of tea tell the invisible beautiful Lady about autumn, its busy creatures and plants, and about spirits that sometimes haunt the land looking for resting places. Their mother listened with tender astonishment. Parents in a story circle imagined Lord and Lady Thaw, friends of Lady Spring and all her court, who dance elegantly in puddles and old snowdrifts. You might tell a playful story about thaw folk and their 'children'.

After an icy, cold winter, another mother who was experimenting with spring stories, wanted to depict the long sleep of early spring. Her imagination produced a wise crow hunched, patiently waiting on an island in the middle of a frozen lake. Only when this wintry bird flew a long journey to Lady Spring and tapped at her window, did she waken in wonder in her lacy bed. As she rose she changed colors. When at last she stepped outside, her footsteps turned the earth green; where she bent to touch it, purple and yellow crocuses sprang up. Her footsteps led her in her flowing mantle to old Winter and his court. She sang a song to him and he tossed out the last of his snowflakes and gravely departed to his arctic retreat. Both she and her children felt that this story had helped to warm the weather at last.

April in northern Europe, America and Canada is a powerful month of muddy transformations. Children need stories about

what springs up unexpectedly like jack-in-the-box – realistic tales about newly born animals and their adventures come naturally. Yet at seven years of age children have a growing affinity for moral realism. A father told his sons about a boy who found a nest of eggs with little pecking sounds stirring inside them. As one cracked slightly open the boy felt pity for the hard work of the little creature. He reached enthusiastically into the nest and opened one of the shells, but the exposed little creature soon curled up and died. The boy cried bitterly while his granddad explained, 'Every chick must do its own peckin'.

A mother inspired by a bright spring morning determined to tell a story of the beginning of everything for her children. She wrapped up completely with them outdoors under a big blanket. Mother and children wriggled together and then lay still for a timeless time. She took a big breath. 'In the beginning,' she heard herself saying 'in the very beginning there was nothing, nothing, nothing.' After a long pause she whispered, 'Then Creation began – and there was – a Cow.' In the story that followed, everything emerged from the Cow: birds, worms, flowers, children, houses... Several days afterward the mother discovered a collection of creation tales from many lands – and read them aloud to her children. Wonderful and fascinating as these were, they did not cause such a satisfying depth of wonder as when this story arose for them, freshly, out of the ground of her own soul.

In a similar mood, a friend told me recently that several children came to stay over night with her son, who was turning seven in April. She and her husband were overwhelmed at first by their wild spring energy, but soon they had devised a plan. She lit a candle ceremoniously. Then she asked the children to wind themselves up tightly in their blankets and sleeping bags. They squirmed about wildly, happy and content as she told them about a caterpillar that searched for food until one day he felt himself to be changing – and spun himself into a shining cocoon. He sensed that when he woke up, much later, he would have glorious wings. Soon all the children were sound asleep, nourished by her voice and the picture language of the story she had told. Breakfast with the 'butterfly children' next morning was unexpectedly peaceful.

Because changes in springtime are so intense, it can be helpful to choose one or two powerful transformation stories and to tell and play them out again and again. Notice what draws the attention of your child. Is it an ant, the old root of an oak tree, pigeon dung, a colorful butterfly, melting frost? Carefully match your words with loving respect to these realities in the stories you tell. Read *The Princess and The Goblin*, *The Princess and Curdie* or *The Golden Key* by George MacDonald. These and many other of his tales portray entities who have participated in life through long ages. Like the mountains and forests in which they live, these beings are powerful representatives of wisdom. They say few words, yet they know a child's needs exactly.

Summer Stories

In the warmth of summer, our senses open wide through the power of the sun. In many countries it is only then that people can move about freely in nature. Summer is the traditional time for journeying, the archetypal foundation for many of the world's greatest stories. An American home-schooling family, who were usually land-locked in a large suburban town, were able to walk one summer's day along the ocean's edge. Afterward the four children, aged three to eight, made crayon drawings of what they had seen. Their mother bound their drawings into a book and wrote with brightly colored pencils what the children said about each picture. They took turns reading their

Ocean Walk story many times, in their own ways. On future occasions they made memory books of other summer excursions to the homes of friends and relatives – and even of those to various stores, and to their pediatrician. Like this family did, you might write down your child's version of a journey you take together. Combine the child's drawings with a special photograph or preferably drawings that you make, of places you especially enjoy together.

Doubtful about their storytelling powers, a group of parents envisioned 'Mother Summer' as a storyteller to inspire them during the long summer days with their children. They pictured her as voluptuously smiling and rounded, wearing vivid blossoms in her hair and at her bosom, her lap and pockets and baskets full to overflowing with cherries and summer flowers. Having summoned her from their imaginations, they began to sense the kinds of stories she might tell. Under the summer stars, and at a loss for words at the end of a long summer's day with her children, one of these mothers asked with bravado and great curiosity: 'What story might great Mother Summer have for us tonight?' She was surprised when what came to her seemed pure inspiration. The story was about a shepherd who, grazing his young animals by night, learned to love the summer constellation of The Ram. The story piqued her curiosity, and began a study of all the constellations and their stories that has lasted to this day in her family.

To speak of the consistent roles of natural things gives children a sense of trust in our universal journey, throughout which all are related and must give to one another. Every creature, plant and stone performs tasks which serve our lives. Summer with its expansive warmth is a natural time to nurture warm gratitude for all living things through the stories you tell. A cheerful worm winds through the soil all day, eating and improving it. 'Thank you worm,' said a little boy I overheard recently, 'That is not how

I would like to spend my day, but you are doing good work.'
Summer stimulates creative spirit, awakening music, dance, painting and poetry. To honor a birthday boy a family wrote a story in simple verse about a growing flower. Parents and young children came to the celebration. After they had recited and acted out their little rhymed story, they paraded around the five-year-old birthday flower-child with xylophone, wooden flutes, thumb piano, triangle and drums.

A group of home-schooling families went to the mines every summer, sometimes traveling long distances with their children to spend time in the cool earth digging for treasures. On the road and during their rest periods the mothers and fathers had decided to tell great old fairy tales that portray goodness and hard work resulting in rich rewards. One of the stories they chose was *Tom Thumb* in which a tiny fellow survives his hard, diminutive life with good spirit. Other favorites were *The Wishing Table, The Donkey and The Stick* and a Scandinavian tale, *The Golden Castle in the Air* about a youth who chose a little gray donkey rather than a gold or silver horse to help him on his way. As they went along the miners admired many rock formations above and below the earth and tales of gnomes and other helpers of the earth also gave the children great delight. Small and diligent, gnomes that live, mysteriously invisible, in close relationship with stones, gravity, and the circulatory currents of the earthy underworld, are pictured in middle European imagination wearing strong boots and pointed hats, like dowsing rods, to help them keep their balance. They can move and see through rocks and perceive the qualities of precious stones. Through these stories the children became sensitive little geologists and, like the potent little gnomes, they learned to respect the qualities and location of stones, the energy packed into jewels. They tried to sense if certain trees and plants were being helped or hindered invisibly by the presences of gnomes.

You might draw or sew one or more gnome like dwarfs, perhaps giving colorful stones for them to care for in little sacks. With your children you might try to imagine ceremonies the earth has been keeping with them through billions of years.

In many spiritual traditions, one of the highest rewards for a good life is to hear and understand the voices of animals or sea-creatures. Fairy tales such as *The Goose Girl* and *Faithful John* portray unusual characters who have received this gift. In George MacDonald's *The Golden Key*, a young girl enters a wood and discovers that her ears have been opened to astonishing conversations amongst plants and animals. To tell such spiritually open stories in summer awakens s subtle perceptions in both our own and the children's hearing.

Storytelling with the Moon

Stories can help young children begin to prepare for adult participation in the lunar rhythms that have influenced human imagination since time immemorial. We can mark the phases of the moon on our storyteller's calendar with deep respect for this radiant, magnetic presence that has drawn forth many of the greatest stories from human beings.

In the moonlight, memory stirs; voices call from the future. Among people more open to the influences of nature, ceremonies are often scheduled in harmony with her. As the moon opens our senses, stories which speak of enhanced sensitivity are reassuring to children. Waiting and watching for the moon to be full is a wholesome activity for them. To help children relate to its fullness during moon times a grandmother in a storytelling circle shared with us that she liked to bake and glaze round cookies or buns with her grandchildren, or slice apples, pears and other fruits crosswise to make juicy, edible little full moons. Their forms shone when they were placed on her favorite plate, which was blue as the night sky.

The moon helps imagination weave finer listening to the truth of the natural worlds. With your children you might create a story circle, bringing dolls, pets, and favorite playthings, careful to make a space of honor for you, the storyteller. Place in the center of this circle a seasonal object such as a flower, fruit or a crystal, or fill a glass bowl with white stones from a favorite shore. Nature's eloquence can speak through you during moon-bright nights; clouds gather and planets convene; animals speak of human beings they fear or love; trees sing of when they were little, and little trees call to the stars to help them grow. On the evening of a full moon a mother gathered her restless 'pixilated' children, wrapped them with her in an old blanket and crooned as they sat together in the moonlit room. Then very tentatively she began a story: *Once when the moon was very full, three little elves, light as feathers, jumped out of hiding in search of fun.* She received their full attention.

Young children who are in the moon's sway can experience an increased sense of vulnerability and exposure to what is hidden; chaotic fears can surface – dreams of beasts who want to eat them, or trolls who want to play with them. Through the picture language of your stories you can help them develop a sense of mastery over these shadowy presences. Your stories can include characters who become surprised by strengths of which they were unaware, perhaps through whistling, or learning to sing or shout magical words.

As spring approached a mother wrote a story for her growing three and six-year-old boys. They had been sleeping more deeply than usual under the full moon.

Once there was a sleeping seed. The little seed turned in its bed. 'Where am I?' The seed sent down roots in earthlight and grew up toward another light. Grandmother Moon saw the little seed. She sang a song and a pathway opened for the seed to the light.

The moon offers a benevolent, loving gaze we all need as we move into new territories of physical and emotional growth. The story concluded: 'The new little plant poked through. "I feel so different today," it sighed joyfully.' The author of this story told her circle of parent storytellers that the children were very content with it. The six-year-old did not ask, 'Mom, is that story really true?' She said she could feel the blessing of the story as it welled up through her: by focusing on the life of a seed she had expressed many aspects of their lives. You also might tell the adventures of seeds under the watchful gaze of Grandmother Moon. Or tell a story about a mustard plant that remembers when it was once a seed, or about the moon's journey through the night sky. Lyrical enjoyment is the birthright of children. As you inspire your children with your own wonder and attention, together you become more fully part of the truth of things.

6 Family and Community Storytelling

All around us we see the breaking of the bond of heart and mind.
Joseph Chilton Pearce

Useful Guidelines

Your commitment to tell stories will gradually change your life with your children in many ways. When in doubt you may wish to consider the following.

1. Each story told for your family inspires the next.

2. Silence deepens the power of listening.

3. Accept that sometimes you may experience reticence and modesty, and a desire that others do the storytelling for you.

4. When you write a schedule for storytelling and keep to it, even when upset, tired, or baffled by circumstances, you will reap many benefits.

5. Anger, impatience, and self-effacement can be transformed by a good story.

6. Telling yourself, 'Normal busy parents haven't time for this' thwarts your innate ability to offer children what they need.

7. Your lack of experience and sense of inadequacy, or any other distractions can be usefully developed into story characters.

8. Enjoy how good it feels to overcome a reluctance to tell stories and notice how your creativity engages the children.

9. Remember what your commitment to storytelling can bring: regular focused time with your children without distractions; pleasure at looking forward to the next story time which is already scheduled into your day and week; the sense of growing closeness in your family; the knitting of old bonds and new; growing interest and respect for other families; growing creativity of your children, reflecting your own; and closer relationships and creative resources for times of trouble and discouragement.

10. The only way to become the storyteller you are is to practice this art. Your heartfelt storytelling activities will promote health, happiness and love. If you are convinced of this, you will achieve your goals.

The Human Tribe

Storytelling helps young children with their inherent tribal instincts to begin to hold a vision of well-being for themselves and the whole earth. It can help them experience the fundamental security of belonging to an extended family. Until quite recently the youngest children were brought up and educated at home with their older brothers and sisters. Because families today tend to be smaller, often with only one child, there is a pervasive nostalgia for close-knit, multi-generational family life. Children breathe a deeper weave of life with tales that portray the lives of human and animal families. The popularity of the books written by Laura Ingalls Wilder stems in great part from our deep need to experience that each individual can be bound delightfully both to family and to the larger community. Longed for and loved by many children, her books show a hardy pioneer family with moral integrity who successfully meet challenges together.

In contrast to realistic historical vignettes of family life, fairy tales tend to portray an individual's striving to become more strong, complete and loving. Both kinds of stories are important to growing children, who have the constant challenge of sharing with and contributing to others, and at the same time learning to be an individual who can stand alone.

To create more of a sense of community, several busy and hard-working mothers and fathers, with children of about the same ages, decided to help one another. Three afternoons a week these families took turns making the evening meal for one another in their own kitchens, so that the other families could benefit from a less pressured evening. With pleasure and growing familiarity, their children gathered in one another's homes after school. Each presiding cook, by previous agreement among the families, told the children a nutritious story or two as the communal dinner was cooking; the families decided together upon guidelines for the meals and stories they would share with one another. When it was time to eat the evening meal, each family fetched their own portions of food home. Gradually everyone associated good food with good stories, as the children shared with their parents and older brothers and sisters the stories they had heard.

Another group of parents decided to take their children, ages one year to fourteen, on a walk of several miles to raise money for hungry and homeless people in their inner-city. Bringing along plenty of food and water, the youngest sometimes in arms or in pushcarts, they determined together that they would finish the whole walk through a maze of city streets, even if it took the whole day and night. As the day went on the parents made up stories about the myriads of people who were walking with them, trying to imagine their lives running marathon races or overcoming adversity; in the midst of their stories, they cheered on the stragglers. These vigorous families repeated the endurance test for several years as the children grew up. Although the journeys were taken for fun and to teach compassion, one mother says several years later, 'I think these walks started a tradition in our family of recognizing that the whole story includes discomfort and strong will. It went right into our feet to keep going, as in the fairy tales, and to look for positive endings.'

One of the strong-willed mothers who took these walks with her four children, responded to a sign: 'Visit us – love is ageless', and decided to take them along to a shelter for the elderly. Their weekly visits gave the family insight into the far spectrum of life. Many of the people who lived there grew to love the mother and children and to look forward to the music they played on their instruments, their singing and the little poems and stories they brought to share with them. 'At first the children were too young to verbalize the reality of friendship and they sometimes wanted to hurry, but once they were there it all became meaningful,' said the mother. At night, as the children slept, or early in the morning before they awoke, she would write down what the old folks had said and done during their visits with them. After a time, with genuine respect and affection, she entitled the book 'Our Elderly Friends', leaving extra pages for adding more anecdotes. She made copies, with the children's colorfully decorated covers, for the families of these elders, the staff of the home, and for others who sometimes visited there. As the people died during the several years they continued with their visits, the mother took special care with her children to write delightful descriptions honoring their lives as they had come to know them.

At holiday time, a family with four children aged three to ten decided to invite their friends, including babies and grandparents, for an evening of storytelling. Everyone they invited wanted to come, and soon their little living room was packed to overflowing. The excited motley group began to sing songs which the older children had learned to play on their various instruments; these provided musical interludes throughout the evening. A child was instructed to ceremoniously place a beautiful simple stone in the center of the crowded room. 'Whoever picks up the stone will be the storyteller,' announced the mother in a clear strong voice as she picked up the stone and beautifully told the first story. This was the beginning: everyone who wished to took the stone and spoke. Each person was listened to with good humor until, after one final round of song, they piled to the dining table for refreshments. Then and there a tradition was born. The communal atmosphere satisfied in them all a deep need. For several more years, as the children in these families grew up together, they met regularly for their Storytelling Evening. Both children and adults grew in confidence during these gatherings, developing their expression and taste in stories. A sense of security pervaded the group even when visitors from other 'tribes' occasionally listened.

During a long hot summer, a group of children and parents I know well created a similar communal spirit in their multi-racial urban neighborhood. They decided to stage a play in their favorite small backyard with its ramshackle garage. They had often enjoyed acting and making games from folk tales discovered in library books. Their first formal production, a Native American tale entitled *The Rough-face Girl*, was so successful that the children continued putting on neighborhood performances together for ten years. The youngest member was not yet two years old when the group began. As the 'announcer' for the first production, she toddled comfortably to the front of the audience to shout with total joy: 'Welcome to our play.' From the beginning, each child was fully involved in choosing the story or play, developing the script, taking parts, designing and building the sets, and making costumes. A relaxed approach permitted each child to voice his or her opinions, and to make decisions about every aspect of each production. They chose a name for their troupe – 'The Backyard Players'. Planning to base each production upon great stories they knew, each year as preparations for their next production began they patiently read the chosen story many times together. They made sure the script they wrote included every child. The youngest children were helped by the older ones, and the group learned to delegate responsibilities and roles that allowed everyone to take a part. At first they were helped by two mothers, with great love for their children and for the theater. Eventually several more parents contributed their skills. The children made tickets for these productions and invited parents and friends. At first all this was for their own enjoyment, but as they realized the benefits of this kind of sharing, they wanted to inspire similar performances in other neighborhoods. After six years the group presented their first abridged Shakespearean production of *As You Like It*. The youngest child among them, who by then was eight years old, took one of the major roles and was the first to memorize all her lines.

Recognizing the powerful leaven of storytelling and imaginative play in neighborhoods, a resourceful grandmother, who lives in a complex, noisy urban area, decided to take action in a different way. She made two storytelling dolls, much as she had made for her own children when they were very small, distilling into them all the qualities which young children have in their best moments. Thinking of the youngest listeners, she used the finest of natural materials and colors and named the dolls Obie and Oba. Then she made posters and sent invitations, and took care to set up a story space in her house with beautiful things to nourish the children's attention to the story: flowers, a candle, a crystal, an evocative piece of cloth. She, the dolls and the children formed a triangle: a story space within which she said, 'We imagined the story together.'

Her story framework was always the same. When the children and their mothers, sitters or other caretakers arrived, she cautioned them, 'Please step softly. My little ones are sleeping.' When all were seated on pillows and a soft carpet, she taught the children a song to awaken the dolls from their naps, and told them they had guests. Then she would settle Obie and Oba together in a chair and ask them what story they would like to hear. The storyteller enjoyed greeting everyone, especially a birthday child if there was one, the grandparents, and, of course, all the other beloved dolls who had come. 'What's that you said, Oba? But who is that? - that's Tim's grandfather!' She took care her words and gestures were as if she were interacting with a child. She usually had planned the story she was going to tell, but sometimes the composition of the group required a last-minute change of plans. The dolls helped her to listen intuitively each time to what was needed by the whole group. If she was interrupted with loud and restless comments: 'They're only dolls! She didn't *really* say that!' the storyteller had a ready answer: 'Of course, we are playing! This is what we are playing!'

At intermission she quietly served refreshments for everyone that were a reflection of something in her stories: cakes in the shape of sun or moon or magical boots; juice the color of roses. After a short intermission, a small elf would appear to start a little argument with the dolls about which story would be next. She wanted to finish before they were tired, while they might be wishing for more. When it was time to stop, the dolls procrastinated, as children often do, until at last she sang, tucked them in and blew out the candle. Fingers to her lips, she and the elf asked the children to go quietly away. Despite the honking traffic outside the window, this gentle and harmonious storytelling routine worked very well for everyone, and led to many good conversations with parents about child care.

Believing that stories can transform social occasions, a friend with two young children, who was about to celebrate her fortieth birthday, decided to invite an experienced storyteller into her small house and ragged garden for a celebration. For various personal reasons, she requested that the story be based on the theme of loyalty. Along with the adults and babysitters came a whole range of youngsters from age two to sixteen. In the garden was a swinging wooden bench, another more tangible birthday gift to herself and her family. Wearing a quieting green garment, the storyteller sat on the bench and played a simple melody on a wooden recorder to gather their attention. At last the whole hullabaloo of a party, at least fifty people together with some of their pets, had assembled on the grass. The storyteller strummed a soothing open-stringed instrument, hummed a simple melody – and began in a powerful voice:

Once upon a time there lived a great king.

The king's messenger in the story decreed:

Hear ye. Hear ye. The time is come again to quest for the Great Pookaseeka. This creature lives on the far side of the Dark Forest, the Endless Flood, the Valley of the Wild Winds and beyond the Fiery Gap. Whoever dares the quest must brave these four tests and you must go two or more together, or you shall surely fail. Before you start, please honor your beloved King by pledging perfect loyalty to one another, no matter how challenging your journey may become. If indeed you attain the Pookaseeka, look you very well to it. Perhaps it will give you a boon, a gift to cherish on your return journey and forever more. Remember all that happens on your journey, both going and returning; if indeed you return, your King and his court will hear your tale.

Then the storyteller stood up and said in a different kind of voice:

Now choose your friends carefully, three or four together. Of course, pets may help. Let an adult be in each group. Pledge your loyalty firmly and truly and only then you may begin the quest. The house and all the garden here are yours to become your story ground. The cellar may become the Dark Wood and this fence here the Forest's edge.

That puddle may become the Endless Flood. Follow faithfully the path of the Holy Quest from Wood to Lake to Valley to Gap. If ever you are in distress, call for help and Helpers will surely come, through the gifts of your true imagination, and bring you safely through your perilous trials and tests. These may be angels in disguise, birds, worms, wizards or cats. In story time twenty minutes can be a year and a day. Remember without fail that help shall surely come in your trials when you call for it. When you hear music sounding, return here to tell your adventures. After the telling of the quests the King will set a great feast. All may freely partake who are truly loyal friends throughout their adventures.

The groups formed: a father and his children, grandparents and godchildren, three mothers together, children and babysitters with eager dogs on leashes, cats, and kittens in arms. Each group in their own ways, playfully, passionately and solemnly pledged loyalty for the journey. Shouts, calls, groans and many adventures later, the storyteller sounded the music for the return, and resumed the storyteller's role. Some came slowly, others quickly; with wonder and glee, they made their way back to the throne of the King. Seeing his people return from their quests stronger and more radiant than before, the King of their story was most pleased. It was his pleasure to hear their adventures told. Each group appointed one storyteller to stand before the group and recount their tales.

After this celebration, which lasted about an hour, abundant food flowed. The storyteller mingled to hear more of the trials and accomplishments of their quests. The clear structure for the journey had given each group a way to inspire one another, and to return full of their experiences for the telling. This playfully communal, archetypal journey, and its rhythmic wholeness, had nurtured even the youngest guests.

I like to imagine a world in the new millennium in which wise and playful storytelling surrounds all little children; where of their own initiative every family that enjoys television and computers agrees to have a day without them at least every now and again. On this day a silence grows and flourishes in and around the house. A natural yearning for storytelling grows. Family and special friends gather around candles, inviting the spirit of the whole human family to join with them. A song or two is sung; someone plays an instrument: a child's violin, a father's harmonica or grandfather's banjo. A parent storyteller begins, perhaps holding a wonderfully empty book, until an original tale or a great, old, familiar tale has been heard, without interruption, from beginning to end. Well-crafted stories come from personal experiences, perhaps remembered by older family members from their own childhoods. A child tells a story learned at school. All are heard with love and respect. Then one last song, and gratitude to all the stories, followed by a space of quiet listening for the story-songs of the wise old earth and skies: the moon, the sun and planets, and the far and twinkling stars. Then supper and bed, in a delightfully satisfying hush...

Acknowledgments

I am grateful to Martin Large and Hawthorne Press for the invitation to write this book, and to John Docherty who, on a windy sea-ledge in Wales, improved so much of it. I cherish everyone, young and old who influenced this book, many of them met through the international Waldorf School movement. There are too many to mention here. I hope they know who they are – Brother Blue and Ruth Hill, my mother, Helen Dann Stringer, Teddy Parker, Gisela Bittleston, Carol and Ifeanyi Menkiti, Guy Peartree, Miriam Ziegler, Betty Peck, Anna Rainville, Sharon Bredlau, Charlotte Haas, Mariko Valbracht, Barbara Damron, Ethelwyn Frank, Anne di Giovanni, Suzanne Down, Kristin Tulimiero, Deborah Bogart, Katrina Kenison, Colin McNaughton, Bayard and Kerry Brokaw, Ben Edwards, Larry and Karen Carter, Ashley and Kristin Ramsden, Martha and Dirk Kelder, Heide Scheuer, Julia Galginaitis, Kathleen van der Weerd, Mary Haydon, Marion Swatton, Nim de Bruyne, Francis Edmunds, Margaret Meyercourt, Lies Nottrot ...

Resources For Each Chapter

Some books and resources to guide and support storytelling with young children

1. Spinning and Weaving a Storyteller's Mantle

Harwood, A.C. 1958. *The Recovery of Man in Childhood*. Anthroposophic Press: Hudson, NY.

Kuhlewind, Georg. 1998. *From Normal to Healthy: Paths to the Liberation of Consciousness*. Lindesfarne: Great Barrington.

Opie, Iona and Peter. 1999. *Puffin Book of Nursery Rhymes*. Puffin.

Patterson 1999. *Beyond the Rainbow Bridge,* Michaelmas Press: Amesbury .

Pearce, Joseph Chilton 1992. *Evolution's End: Claiming the Potential of Our Intelligence* Harper: New York;1977. *The Magical Child*. Dutton: New York. *The Magical Child Matures.*

Pyle, Howard 1965. *The Wonder Clock*. Dover: New York.

Salter, Joan 1987. *The Incarnating Child*. Hawthorn: Stroud.

Sanders, Barry 1995. *A is for ox: The Collapse of Literacy and the Rise of Violence in an Electronic Age*. Vintage: New York.

Sawyer, Ruth 1962. *The Way of the Storyteller*. Viking: New York.

Shedlock, Marie 1952. *The Art of the Storyteller*. Dover: New York

Soesman, Albert. 1999. *Our Twelve Senses: How Healthy Senses Refresh the Soul*. Hawthorn: Stroud.

Udo de Haes, Daniel 1986. *The Young Child: Creative Living with 2-4 Year Olds*. Floris: Edinburgh.

2. A Storyteller's Trove of Treasures: Memory and Imagination

Akaret, Robert U. & Daniel Klein 1991. *Family Tales, Family Wisdom: How to Gather the Stories of a Lifetime and Share them with your Family*. William Morrow & Co.: New York.

Davis, Donald 1993. *Telling Your Own Stories*. August House: Little Rock: Arkansas.

Kenison, Katrina 2000. *Mitten Strings for God: Reflections for Mothers in a Hurry*. Warner: New York.

Livo, Norma & Sandra Rietz 1987. *Storytelling Activities*. Libraries Unlimited: Englewood, Colorado.

Maguire, Jack 1985. *Creative Storytelling: Choosing, Inventing and Sharing Tales for Children*. Yellow Moon: Cambridge, Massachusetts. *The Power of Personal Storytelling: Spinning Tales to Connect with Others*. Jeremy Tarcher: New York.

3. A Storyteller's Trove of Treasures: Play

Berger, Petra. *Feltcraft: Making Dolls, Gifts and Toys*. Floris: Edinburgh.

Brooking-Payne, Kim. 1998. *Games Children Play*. Hawthorn: Stroud.

Cox, Marion. *Cinderella: Three Hundred and Forty-five Variants*.

Fryer, Jane 1999. *The Mary Frances Sewing Book*. Philadelphia: John Winston.

Hamilton, Martha & Mitch Weiss 1996. *Stories in My Pocket*. Fulcrum: Golden, Colorado.

Harrison, Annette. 1992. *Easy-to-Tell-Stories for Young Children*. National Storytelling Press: Jonesborough, Tennessee.

Holt, David and Mooney, Bill 1994. *Ready to Tell Tales*. August House.: Little Rock.

Mayer, Gladys. 1983. *Mystery of Colour: How Healthy Senses Refresh the Soul*. Anthroposophic Press: Hudson.

National Storytelling Association 1994. *Tales as Tools*. National Storytelling Press: Jonesborough Tennessee.

Opie, Iona and Peter. 1992. *Oxford Nursery Rhyme Book*. Oxford University Press: Oxford. *Singing Games*. Oxford University Press: Oxford.

Ouseley, S.G.J. 1949. *Color Meditations*. Fowler: Romford.

Poulsson, Emilie. *Finger Plays for Nursery & Kindergarten*. Dover: New York.

Reinckens, Sunnhild. *Making Dolls*. Floris: Edinburgh.

Rosenbluth, Vera. 1997. *Keeping Family Stories Alive: Discovering & Recording the Stories and Reflections of a Lifetime*. Hartley & Marks: Vancouver, British Columbia.

Shedlock, Marie. 1951. *The Art of the Storyeller*. Dover: New York.

Sinclair, Anita 1995. *The Puppetry Handbook*. Richard Lee: Castlemaine VIC, Australia.

'The Temperaments' in 1983. *Lifeways.* Gudrun Davy & Bons Voors (eds.) Hawthorn: Stroud.

Thompson, Stith. 1997. *The Folktale.* University of California Press: Berkeley.

Totline Staff 1994. *1001 Rhymes and Finger Plays.* Warren: Everett, Washington.

Willwerth, Kundry. *Let's Dance and Sing: Story Games for Children.* Mercury Press: Spring Valley, New York.

Wiseman, Herbert & Sydney Northcote. *The Clarendon Books of Singing Games.* Oxford University Press: London.

4. Stories For Growth and Change

Baltuck, Naomi 1995. *Multicultural Folk Tales about Stories and Storytellers.* Linnet: New Haven.

Bennett, William. 1993. *The Book of Virtues.* Simon & Schuster: New York.

Berger, Thomas and Petra 1999. *The Gnome Craft Book.* Floris : Edinburgh.

Bettelheim, Bruno 1976. *The Uses of Enchantment: The Meaning and Importance of Fairy Tales.* Knopf: NY.

Brooking-Payne, Kim. *Games Children Play.* Hawthorn: Stroud, Gloucestershire.

Coles, Robert 1997. *The Moral Intelligence of Children.* Plume: New York.

Davy, Gudrun & Bons Voors (eds.) 1983. *Lifeways: Working with Family Questions.* Hawthorn: Stroud.

Druitt, A., M. Rowling, C. Fynes-Clinton. 2000. *Birthday Book.* Hawthorn: Stroud.

Eliot, Alexander 1976. *The Universal Myths.* Penguin: New York.

Fenner, Pamela J. and Karen L. Rivers. *Waldorf Student Reading List.* Michaelmas Press.

Fraiberg, Selma 1959 *The Magic Years.* Scribner's: New York.

Gersie, Alida 1991. *Storytelling in Bereavement.* Jessica Kingsley: London.

Guroian, Vigen. 1998. *Tending the Heart of Virtue: How Classic Stories Awaken a Child's Moral Imagination.* Oxford University Press: New York.

Heuscher, Julius. 1974. *A Psychiatric Study of Myths and Fairy Tales: Their Origin, Meaning and Usefulness.* Charles Thomas: Springfield, Illinois.

Kenison, Katrina. 2000. *Mitten Strings for God.* Warner: New York.

Lehrer, Warren. 1995. *Brother Blue.* Bay Press: Seattle.

Livo, Norma J 1994. *Who's Afraid? Facing Children's Fears with Folktales.* Englewood, Colorado: Libraries Unlimited, Inc. 1996. *Troubadour's Storybag: Musical Folktales of the World.* Fulcrum: Golden Colorado.

MacDonald, Margaret Read 1995. *The Parents' Guide to Storytelling: How to Make Up New Stories and Retell Old Favorites.* Harper Collins: NewYork. 1999. *Earthcare.*

Mellon, Nancy 1998. *The Art of Storytelling.* Element: Boston.

Meyer, Rudolf 1988. *The Wisdom of Fairy Tales.* Floris: Edinburgh.

Pearson, Jenny 1996. *Discovering the Self Through Drama and Movement.* Jessica Kingsley: London.

Rudman, Marsha Kabakow 1995. *Children's Literature: An Issues Approach.* Longman: New York.

Sendak, Maurice. *Where the Wild Things Are. Outside Over There.* Harper Collins: New York.

von Franz, Maria 1982. *Interpretation of Fairy Tales.* 1980. *The Meaning of Redemption Motifs in Fairy Tales.* Spring Publications: Dallas.

Tolkien, J.R.R. 1964. 'On Fairy Stories' in *Tree and Leaf.* George Allen&Unwin: London.

Whiteley, Opal. *Opal: The Journal of an Understanding Heart.* Adapted by Jane Boulton. Three Rivers Press: NY.

5. Stories Through the Seasons

Aulie, Jennifer and Meyercourt, Margaret. *Autumn.* Wynstones Press: Stourbridge. Also in the same series, *Winter Spring, Summer, Gateways, Spindrift.*

Boone, J. Allen. 1954. *Kinship with All Life.* Harper: San Francisco.

Caduto, Michael and Joseph Bruchac. 1991. *Keepers of the Animals: Native American Stories and Wildlife Activities for Children.* Fulcrum: Golden, Colorado. 1988 *Keepers of the Earth: American Stories and Environmental Activities for Children.* Fulcrum: Golden, Colorado. 1990. *Keepers of the Night.* Fulcrum: Golden, Colorado.

Fynes-Clinton, Christine, Ann Druitt, Marije Rowling. *All Year Round.* Hawthorn: Stroud.

Hobsen, *The Work of the Fairies.*

Knijpenga, Siegwart. *Stories of Saints.* Floris: Edinburgh.

Krupp, E.C. 1991. *Beyond the Blue Horizon: Myths and Legends of the Sun, Moon, Stars and Planets.* Oxford University Press: Oxford.

Leeuwen, M.V. & J. Moeskops 1999. *The Nature Corner.* Floris: Edinburgh.

Milord, Susan 1996. *Tales of the Shimmering Sky: Ten Global Folktales*; 1999. *Hands Around the World : 365 Creative Ways to Encourage Cultural Awareness and Global Respect;* 1998. *Bird Tales from Near and Far.* Williamson: Charlotte, Vermont.

Neumann, Erich 1954. *The Great Mother.* Bollingen Series No.47. New York: Pantheon Books.

Pogacnik, Marco 1995. *Nature Spirits & Elemental Beings: Working with the Intelligence in Nature.* Findhorn Press: Forres.

Sun Bear & Wabun 1980. *The Medicine Wheel.* Simon and Schuster: New York.

von Heider, W.M. 1999. *Come Unto These Yellow Sands.* Rudolf Steiner College Press: Sacramento.

6. Stories: Weaving Family and Community

Campbell, Laura Ann. 1999. *Storybooks for Tough Times.* Fulcrum: Golden, CO.

Fitzjohn, Sue, Weston, Minda, Large, Judy 1993. *Festivals Together: A Guide to Multi-cultural Celebration.* Hawthorn Press: Stroud, Glos.

MacDonald, Margaret Read 1986. *Twenty Tellable Tales: Audience Participation Folktales for the Beginning Storyteller.* H.W.Wilson.

McAllen, Audrey 1981. *Sleep.* Hawthorn: Stroud.

National Storytelling Association 1994. *Tales as Tools.* The National Storytelling Press: Jonesborough, Tennessee.

Nelson, Gertrude Mueller 1986. *To Dance with God.* Paulist Press: New York.

Pellowski, Anne 1987. *The Family Storytelling Handbook.* Macmillan: New York.

Sanders, Barry 1995. *A Is For Ox: The Collapse of Literacy and the Rise of Violence in an Electronic Age.* Vintage: New York.

Wilder, Laura Ingalls, 1989. *Little House Books.* Harpercollins: New York.

Zipes, Jack 1995. *Creative Storytelling: Building Community, Changing Lives.* Routledge.

Short and Longer Stories Mentioned:

Bates, H.E. 1984. *My Uncle Silas.* Oxford University Press: Oxford.

Baum, Frank. 1992. *The Wizard of Oz.* Knopf, New York.

Beskow, Ella. *Pelle's New Suit.* Floris: Edinburgh.

Carroll, Lewis. 1965. *The Works of Lewis Carroll.* Ed. R.L.Green, London: Spring-Hamlyn.

'Cinderella' in 1972. *The Complete Grimms' Fairy Tales.* Pantheon: New York.

De Paolo, Tomi. *The Legend of Old Befana.* Harcourt, Brace, Javanovish: New York.

Durrell, Gerald. 1962. *My Family and Other Animals.* Rupert Hart-Davis: London.

Ende, Michael. 1984. *The Never-ending Story.* Viking: New York.

'Faithful John'. 1972. *The Complete Grimms' Fairy Tales.* Pantheon: New York.

'Goldilocks and the Three Bears' in Frederick Richardson 1972. *Great Children's Stories.* Rand-McNally: Chicago.

'Grandfather Plants a Turnip Seed' in a manuscript by Anna Rainville 1999. *The Golden Ring.*

'Jorinda and Joringel' in 1972. *The Complete Grimms' Fairy Tales.* Pantheon: New York.

'Jumping Mouse' in Hyemeyohsts Storm 1985. *Seven Arrows.* Ballantine: New York.

Lagerlof, Selma. *The Wonderful Adventures of Nils.* Floris: Edinburgh.

Lewis, C.S.1983. *Chronicles of Narnia.* MacMillan: New York.

Lindgren, Astrid. 1997. *Pippi Longstocking Omnibus.* Viking: New York.

'Little Red Riding Hood' in 1972. *The Complete Grimms' Fairy Tales.* Pantheon: New York.

Longfellow, Henry Wadsworth. 1982. *Song of Hiawatha.* Crown: New York.

'Matilda Who Told Lies' in *Cautionary Tales,* Hillaire Belloc.

MacDonald, George. *The Wise Woman. The Princess and the Goblin. The Princess and Curdie.* (reprints from original editions). Johannesen:

Whitethorn, California; 1967. *The Golden Key.* Struass Farrar Giroux: NY; 1992. *The Golden Key and Other Fairy Tales.* Sunburst: New York.

'Mother Holle' in 1972. *The Complete Grimms' Fairy Tales.* Pantheon: New York.

Ruskin, John. 2000. *The King of the Golden River.* Candlewick:

St. George and The Dragon. Margaret Hodges. 1984. Boston: Little Brown.

'Snow White' in 1972. *The Complete Grimms' Fairy Tales.* Pantheon: New York.

'Sweet Porridge' in 1972. *The Complete Grimms' Fairy Tales.* Pantheon: New York.

'The Ant and the Grasshopper' in *Aesop's Fables.* Michael Hague (ed.) 1985. Holt, Reinhart & Winston: New York.

'The Donkey', in 1972. *The Complete Grimms' Fairy Tales.* Pantheon: New York.

'The Emperor's New Clothes' in Hans Andersen': *42 Tales.* M.R. James trans. 1976. A.S.Barnes: New York.

'The Firebird' in *Russian Fairy Tales.* Aleksandr Afanasev 1976. Pantheon: NY.

'The Frog Prince', in 1972. *The Complete Grimms' Fairy Tales.* Pantheon: New York.

'The Goose Girl' in 1972. *The Complete Grimms' Fairy Tales.* Pantheon: New York.

'The Queen Bee' in 1972. *The Complete Grimms' Fairy Tales.* Pantheon: New York.

'The Rough-face Girl'. Rafe Martin, G.P. Putnam's Sons, New York.

'The Singing Bone' in 1972. *The Complete Grimms' Fairy Tales.* Pantheon: New York

'The Three Billy Goats Gruff' in Virginia Haviland 1985. *Favorite Fairy Tales Told Around the World.* Little, Brown: Boston.

'The Three Little Men in the Wood' in 1972. *The Complete Grimms' Fairy Tales.* Pantheon: New York.

'The Three Little Pigs' in Virginia Haviland 1985. *Favorite Fairy Tales Told Around the World.* Little, Brown: Boston.

'The Waters of Life', in 1972. *The Complete Grimms' Fairy Tales.* Pantheon: New York

'The Wishing Table, The Donkey and the Stick' in 1972. *The Complete Grimms' Fairy Tales.* Pantheon: New York.

'The Wolf and the Seven Little Kids' in 1972. *The Complete Grimms' Fairy Tales.* Pantheon: New York.

'Tom Thumb' in Virginia Haviland 1985. *Favorite Fairy Tales Told Around the World*. Little, Brown: Boston.

'Tom Tit Tot' in Joseph Jacobs,

Travers, P.L. *Mary Poppins.*

Sendak, Maurice. 1988. *Where the Wild Things Are*, 1985. *In The Night Kitchen*; *1981. Outside Over There* Harpercollins: New York.

Vasilissa the Beautful' in *Russian Fairy Tales*, 1980 trans. Robert Chandler. Random: Boston.

Wilder, Laura Ingalls, 1989. *Little House in the Big Woods*. Harpercollins: New York.

Storytelling Networks

LANES League for the Advancement of New England Storytelling P.O. Box 323 Wrentham MA 02093. Website: www.lanes.org.

National Storytelling Network, 116 West Main Street, Jonesborough, TN. 37659 Email: nsn@naxs.net. Website: www.storynet.org

School of Storytelling, Emerson College, Forest Row, East Sussex RH18 5JX England Email: mail@emerson.org.uk Website: www.emerson.org.uk

Scottish Storytelling Centre, The Netherbow, 43-45 High Street, Edinburgh, Scotland EH1 1SR. Tel: 0131-557-5724.

Storytelling Foundation International, 116 West Main Street, Jonesborough, TN. 37659. Tel: 800-952-8392.

Yellow Moon Press, P.O. Box 381316 Cambridge, MA 02238 Email: ymp@tiac.net

Society for Storytelling, PO Box 2344, Reading RG6 7FG, England Tel: 0118 935 1381 Website: www.sfs.org.uk

Other books from Hawthorn Press

Early Years Series

Muddles, Puddles and Sunshine
Your activity book to help when someone has died
Winston's Wish

Muddles, Puddles and Sunshine offers practical and sensitive support for bereaved children. Beautifully illustrated, it suggests a helpful series of activities and exercises accompanied by the friendly character of Bee and Bear.
September 2000; 32pp; 297 x 210mm landscape; colour illustrations; paperback; 1 869 890 58 2

The Genius of Play
Sally Jenkinson

This book is an observation of the tireless imagination of the child when it is allowed to develop naturally, and how this shapes the perceptions of the later adult. It addresses what 'play' is, why it is necessary and its modern difficulties.
Autumn 2000; 128pp; 216 x 138mm; paperback; 1 903458 06 4

Introducing Steiner Waldorf Early Years Education
Lynne Oldfield

From the Foreword by Sally Jenkinson:

'For almost eighty years in as many different contexts and cultures, from the Favelas in Sao Paulo to the townships in South Africa, Steiner Waldorf Education has provided early years care and education for some of the world's children. Described as 'this most modest movement' its kindergartens and schools have consistently striven to give children the highest quality of educational nurturing in their early years. Different kindergartens vary according to local need but what remains constant is a deeply held belief that childhood matters; that the early years are not a phase of life to be rushed through, but a stage of tremendous importance needing to be experienced fully in its own right. Underpinning this book is the conviction that the child's early learning is profound; that *quality* of early experience is every bit as important as *quantity*. It is a book which implicitly acknowledges that the way we learn, as well as what we learn, will set the arrow of our future on its particular course, for better or for worse.'

160pp; 216 x 138mm; paperback; 1 903458 06 4

Helping Children to Overcome Fear
The Healing Power of Play
Russell Evans

Critical illness can cause overwhelming feelings of abandonment and loss. Difficult for adults to face alone, for children the experience is magnified. They have to leave home for an alien hospital world, without the comfort of familiar daily rhythms.

Jean Evans was a play leader who recognised ahead of her time the importance of enabling children to give voice to their feelings, providing opportunities for play and working in partnership with parents. These requirements are now core principles in the training and working practice in the fields of nursery nursing, play therapy, childcare and Paediatrics. Her practical insights embrace:-

- Child development through play and imitation
- Captivating children's interest
- Encouragement as a source of healing
- Practical guidelines for helping children to feel safe and happy
- Dying children and caring parents

Full of touching and useful examples of how Jean applied this in her work, *Helping Children to Overcome Fear* serves to remind us that these principles are relevant not only to the critically ill but can be used to support all children, everywhere.

'Jean Evans was a remarkable woman who worked for many years as a Play Leader at Llandough Hospital looking after critically ill children in the Children's Cancer Unit. She will be remembered as a caring and compassionate companion of the children and their families who were under her care. However, this only tells part of the story, she was brilliantly innovative in her work with the dying child and this, perhaps, is her most lasting legacy as her thoughts and deeds influenced, and still do, the doctors and nurses who look after these children. This book, written by her husband Russell, brings these threads together so that even more people can benefit from Jean's work.'

Dr Roger Verrier Jones
Paediatrician, Llandough Hospital

'This inspirational book should become mandatory reading for Paediatricians and Play Therapists ... indeed any adult who is serious in their desire to be alongside a child needing to face their fear. It gently embraces the skills of respectful listening, creativity and fun – instantly recognisable to a discerning child.'

Julie Stokes, Consultant Psychologist
Founder of Winston's Wish,
a Grief Support Programme for Children

Getting in touch with Hawthorn Press

What are your pressing questions about the early years?
The Hawthorn Early Years Series arises from parents' and educators' pressing questions and concerns – so please contact us with *your* questions. These will help spark new books, workshops or festivals if there is sufficient interest. We will be delighted to hear your views on our Early Years books, how they can be improved, and what your needs are.

Visit our website for details of the Early Years Series and forthcoming books and events:

http://www.hawthornpress.com

Ordering books

If you have difficulties ordering Hawthorn Press books from a bookshop, you can order direct from:

United Kingdom
Scottish Book Source Distribution,
137 Dundee Street, Edinburgh,
EH11 1BG
Tel: 0131 229 6800 Fax: 0131 229 9070

North America
Anthroposophic Press c/o Books International,
PO Box 960,
Herndon, VA 201 72-0960.
Toll free order line: 800-856-8664
Toll free fax line: 800-277-9747

Dear Reader

If you wish to follow up your reading of this book, please tick the boxes below as appropriate, fill in your name and address and return to Hawthorn Press:

 Please send me a catalogue of other Hawthorn Press books.

☐ Please send me details of Early Years events and courses.

Questions I have about the Early Years are:

_____

_____

_____

_____

_____

Name _____

Address _____

_____

_____

Postcode _____ Tel. no. _____

Please return to: Hawthorn Press, Hawthorn House,
1 Lansdown Lane, Stroud, Glos. GL5 1BJ, UK
or Fax (01453) 751138